Crystal Lies
Choices in the New Age

F. LaGard Smith

VINE
BOOKS

Servant Publications
Ann Arbor, Michigan

Vine Books is an imprint of Servant Publications especially designed to serve Evangelical Christians.

Published by Servant Publications
P.O. Box 8617
Ann Arbor, Michigan 48107

Cover design by Michael Andaloro
Cover photograph by Steve Hunt/The Image Bank

89 90 91 92 93 10 9 8 7 6 5 4 3 2 1

ISBN 0-89283-640-7

Dedicated to
My Aunt Mary
Who lives life in simplicity and contentment.

With appreciation to
Jerry E. Jones
Geoffrey Luckock

Contents

ONE

Changing Times in a New Age

NOT SINCE THE RENAISSANCE has there been such potential for sweeping changes in a society's religious and cultural outlook. On the verge of the twenty-first century, the New Age movement promises unparalleled enlightenment and human potential, but portends a return to ancient pagan mysticism and superstition. Never before has a "Christian America" been so severely challenged. Never before have so many people bolted from traditional religions for a human philosophy which calls into question the very foundations of Christianity. Is it a great truth that is being discovered by New Agers, or are New Agers falling victim to crystal lies?

Signs of the New Age movement appear almost everywhere these days. One of the most dramatic indications is found in your local bookstore. Walk into any secular bookstore and you will see New Age sections larger than the separate Religion section, now often shunted off into the back corner. A quick look at the titles gives you a good overview of the eclectic nature of the movement. For example, there are books on psychic channeling, medicinal crystals, past life regression, chakras, cosmic energy fields,

1

holistic healing, parapsychology, dream interpretation, UFO's, extraterrestrials, human potential, mind energy, color healing, out-of-body experiences, and reincarnation. Spiced in with these subjects are books drawing from more traditional Eastern religions: Hinduism, Buddhism, Taoism, even Zoroastrianism.

You will also find the writings of gurus of every stripe, from Bhagwan Shree Rajneesh (who gained fame from his controversial Oregon commune), to Elizabeth Clare Prophet (affectionately known as "Guru Ma"), to Baba Ram Dass (Guru Ram Dass), to Swami Muktananda (who has influenced *est* founder Werner Erhard, singers Diana Ross and John Denver, actresses Marsha Mason and Olivia Hussey, and even former California Governor Jerry Brown). There is also Guru Maharaj Ji (who exploded onto the guru scene at the age of 15 and founded the Divine Light Mission), and Maharishi Mahesh Yogi (founder of TM, the Transcendental Meditation Program).

If you want ties to more traditional Christian themes, they are on the shelves as well. You can learn about the so-called apocryphal gospels or the missing 18 years of Jesus' life. You can find out how the early Christian church supposedly suppressed claimed biblical teachings of reincarnation. For a hefty price, you can also purchase the *Course in Miracles,* which has sold almost half a million copies worldwide. It sounds like Christian teaching, but is New Age from cover to cover.

While you are there, you may want to purchase tarot cards or astrology charts or perhaps even your own neatly packaged crystals. And how could you leave without picking up *Cosmic Cuisine,* an astrological cookbook "bringing every meal into sync with the stars," or *Gay Signs,* an astrological guide for homosexuals, or *Yoga for Self-Healing?*

Best-selling books by actress Shirley MacLaine, the goddess of the New Age movement, have already sold over 8 million copies. *Out On a Limb, Dancing in the Light,* and *It's All in the Playing* have become a cosmic collection of New Age thought, even if many classical New Agers scoff at Ms. MacLaine's popularized and sometimes outrageous version. Most of those who buy her books are only interested in learning about the inside story of a famous actress. They don't realize that they are about to be indoctrinated in New Age philosophy.

Ms. MacLaine's latest book, *Going Within,* promises to teach readers how to use powerful spiritual technologies to become happier, healthier, and more aware. The goal is to reclaim the power to shape lives, to deal with "unfinished business" in relationships at work and at home. The purpose is to center ourselves metaphysically, then to re-create the world beyond the world within. All of this will be accomplished, says Ms. MacLaine, through "soul physics," using tools such as meditation, chanting, and the channeling of the healing energy of light into the body's chakra centers to lift us to the highest possible plane of consciousness.

In case you might have overlooked the drift of these subjects and titles, they are books which once were found under the heading of The Occult. As in witches and witchcraft. As in Satanism. As in spiritism, mysticism, and shamanism. And they are selling in the millions to mainstream America—to your friends at work, to your next-door neighbors, to your fellow Christians at church, and to your children.

Perhaps you have bought them yourself. Perhaps you have even been drawn to their message, which, in a nutshell, is that we are all divine beings with unlimited potential. If so, you are in good company. Millions of Americans have left traditional churches and walked confidently into the New Age of enlightenment, as they see it. Thousands more

remain in traditional churches but have adopted a syncre-
tized blend of Christianity and New Age thought.

NEW AGE IN THE CHURCH

One of the most notable examples of such a blending is
found in the person of Matthew Fox, a Dominican priest
who has mixed his liberal New Age philosophy with Roman
Catholic doctrine. Founder of the Institute in Culture and
Creation Spirituality at Holy Names College in Oakland,
California, Fox has been sentenced to a year of silence by the
Vatican. Fox has come under fire for hiring faculty members
who include a Zen Buddhist and a self-described witch
named Starhawk, who teaches classes on ritual-making and
sexuality, and spirituality in native religions.

The curriculum at Fox's institute emphasizes Christian
mysticism, feminism, and environmentalism—all of which
are key elements of the New Age movement. Fox's response
to the charges against him? "Diversity is one of the riches of
Catholicism, but one wonders if it is being sacrificed for the
sake of conformity and control" (*Los Angeles Times*, October
19, 1988). Amid the "diversity" to which Fox presumably
refers is his belief, as charged by the church, in pantheism—
the view that everything is God and God is everything—
and his belief in the need to feminize the concept of God.

Protestants, too, have found New Age terminology and
philosophy beginning to work its way into Christian
dialogue. A number of well-known evangelists have encouraged Christians to say that we are all gods, like Jesus was a
god; that Jesus never claimed exclusive divinity; that, just as
Jesus said "I am," we too can say with equal confidence, "I
am!"

Whether Catholic or Protestant, traditional Christian
beliefs have been invaded by the New Age movement with
a fierceness not witnessed since pagan practices found their
way into the ritual of the early Christian centuries.

THE NEW AGE'S POPULAR APPEAL

The influence of the New Age movement is not limited to any one social, economic, or religious group. It permeates the whole of society, from top to bottom, from the highly educated to young people not yet out of school, from the wealthy to the less fortunate who live in ghettos. What began as a fad in the sixties—complete with hippies, flower-power, psychedelic drugs, and Indian sitar music—has become the religion of choice in the eighties.

The religion of human potential, seen in programs like *est* (now The Forum) and Lifespring, has grown up. It has come out of the closet, wearing a new look of spirituality. It has become respectable, taking on believed scientific validation. It's no longer a fad involving a few kookie Californians. It is found from coast to coast, and from New York to the Bible Belt. It's everywhere, and it's here to stay.

Not long ago, I received a call from one of the most successful graduates of the law school where I teach. Within five years of his graduation, John (not his real name) had become one of the most outstanding criminal law attorneys in southern California. From there, he ventured out into the business world, and became a wealthy entrepreneur. He had everything anyone might want, except, apparently, peace of mind. But the voice on the other end of the line was filled with excitement. He wanted to take me to lunch and tell me about a new spiritual dimension which he had discovered.

When the day for our lunch arrived, John picked me up in front of the law school in his chauffeur-driven limousine. As we headed down the hill toward the restaurant, John turned to me in all seriousness and said, "LaGard, I've discovered a great truth. We have to get out of our materialism and seek a revolutionary new spiritualism." Struck by the irony of the circumstances, I remember thinking, "What are you saying, John? Should we get out of your limo and walk?"

Over a two-hour lunch, John went into great detail about

his newly-discovered belief system. It had to do with quantum physics, in which subatomic particles show no tendency toward inherent order, contrary to the way in which molecular theories traditionally have explained order in our universe. It posited how, as observers, we affect the very phenomena which we observe, making all observations merely subjective evaluations of what we formerly believed to be objective truths. It was all about relativism, whether in science, nature, or morals. It was about creating our own reality; about our being one with the universe and one with God. For John, traditional religion and its world view was a limiting factor in personal and social progress. We have been blinded by hierarchical views of power and by materialistic notions of our universe. In the spiritual realm, truth is to be found within each of us as we individually view the reality of who we are.

I sat patiently as John excitedly presented me with his great spiritual discovery. It must have disappointed him that I did not catch the dream with equal enthusiasm. In fact, I was greatly amazed that so bright a mind with such potential for true spirituality had come to believe in a counterfeit spirituality. How quickly he had equated relativity in subatomic particles with relativity in moral truth. How easily he had confused true soul-oriented spirituality with what ultimately is an exclusively material view of the nature of man—exactly what he was trying to escape! When man's soul is equated with protons and neutrons, he is no longer a spiritual being.

Worse yet, the look in John's eye and his responses to my probing of his new world view told me that he was no longer open to a search for truth. He had accepted a belief system that, for whatever reasons, had locked him into a closed mind on the subject. If enlightenment is a *process*, he had completed the process and, at least for now, was one of the enlightened ones.

IS THERE NO TRUTH?

I often hear that religion thrives on closed-mindedness. And certainly there is abundant evidence that the church is close-minded on a whole range of issues. But that is to be expected of a belief system which acknowledges absolute moral truth. One often confuses absolute truth with one's own perception of that truth. Yet for those who believe in the relativity of truth or indeed that there is no such thing as truth, open-mindedness ought to be a philosophical hall-mark. Ironically, the insistence that there is no capital "T" truth becomes itself the ultimate truth for those who pay homage to absolute relativism, and invariably leads to a mind closed to any other possibilities.

The difficulty of having any meaningful dialogue with those who accept New Age philosophy is their belief that we must abandon rationality. Western, male-oriented, left-brain rationality is rejected as limiting one's greater aware-ness. In the New Age, it is Eastern, female-oriented, right-brain intuition that really counts. Until we learn to *feel* rather than to *think*, we are told, we will not understand our true nature. We will continue to believe that we could never be God, that we live in a world of evil as well as good, that we often face circumstances over which we have no control, and that we live only once in this plane of existence.

We are told that, if we continue to be led by such church-dictated rationality, we will never recognize our human potential or allow our consciousness the kind of awareness that can bring about world peace to the global community. Spiritual success in the New Age is found in going inward to one's own subjective awareness rather than outward to an external God and to an objective truth about the universe in which we live.

In the sixties, the slogan was, "If it feels good, *do* it." In the New Age of the eighties and nineties, the lure is, "If it feels good, *believe* it." Once feelings become the standard by which all is to be judged, then no longer can there be any significant dialogue. No longer is there a mutual search for truth. In the New Age, there *is* no truth! Your truth is as good as mine; mine is as valid as yours.

New Agers are quick to say that each of us has his or her own truth, but, of course, equally quick to say that traditional Christian belief is misguided, blind, and narrow. It does not comport with "true reality." Denying, as it does, man's divinity, Christianity falls short of enlightened understanding. Christian faith, like compulsive neatness, is said to be the hobgoblin of little minds.

Where, then, do we begin in attempting to sort out truth from fiction, objectivity from subjectivity, biblical teaching from secular philosophy? What common ground do we have? By New Age thinking, even the title of this book has no relevance. If there is no knowable truth, there can be no lies, no deception. Each of us is creating our own reality *about* reality.

With such a conflict in fundamental perceptions, Pilate's question to Jesus is our question as well: What is truth? What is reality? What can we know that we can hang our hats on, that we can live by, indeed, that we can *die* by? What options are available to us in the New Age? And what will be our choices?

In this book, we will match Christian faith squarely with the New Age movement. However, Christian faith is not to be confused with the teachings of the church, which all too often is couched in terms of human tradition and legislated ritual. For our purposes, Christian faith is the heart of the gospel of Jesus Christ as revealed in Holy Scripture.

Naturally, not everyone agrees that we should look to Scripture for the answers to life's questions. But there must be *some* point of departure for dialogue, and the very fact that you are reading this book probably indicates your familiarity with and respect for the teachings of Scripture.

Despite their rejection of a personal, creative God who has revealed his mind to man through the pages of holy writ, even those who are in the New Age movement appeal to Scripture in an attempt to justify such beliefs as reincarnation. If only there could be a mutual acceptance of the apostle Paul's affirmation that

> All Scripture is God-breathed and is useful for teaching, rebuking, correcting and training in righteousness, so that the man of God may be thoroughly equipped for every good work. (2 Timothy 3:16, 17)

A consistent, serious appeal to Scripture would resolve easily enough the differences between Christian belief and New Age philosophy.

Does the New Age movement bring us closer to God, or does it deceive us when it tells us that we *are* God? Does it imbue us with unlimited human potential, or does it deceive us into believing we have power belonging only to God? Does New Age thought bring us to an enlightened Age of Aquarius or take us back to an age of magic and superstition? In the end, what shall we choose: biblical truth or crystal lies?

TWO

I Am God—You Are God

U PON MY ARRIVAL AT THE ATLANTA AIRPORT after an exhausting flight from London, I called the producer at the "700 Club" to arrange final details for an appearance on a program regarding the New Age movement. It had been a busy talk-show circuit ever since I wrote *Out On a Broken Limb*, a response to actress Shirley MacLaine's own *Out On a Limb* and her more recent New Age books. The voice on the line informed me that Ms. MacLaine was to be in Virginia Beach the same weekend I was to arrive there for the "700 Club," presenting the first of her "Connecting With Your Higher Self" seminars. I immediately called the number advertised for the seminar and signed myself up for the two-day event, to the tune of $300 on my VISA card.

Assuming that at that price there would be only a handful of seminar participants, I became concerned that Ms. MacLaine might recognize me among the faces before her. My picture had been on the back of *Out On a Broken Limb*, which I knew she had read. I wanted to hear what she would say at her seminars, but I did not want my presence to be confrontational. As it turned out, my fears were unmerited. When I arrived at the hotel where the seminar was to be held, wearing my hurriedly purchased jogging outfit and carrying a borrowed pillow (the required outfit and

11

equipment for the day), I found myself among 800 other people. So much for Ms. MacLaine's recognizing my face among the crowd!

THE GREAT LIE

Naturally, there was great pushing and shoving to get the best seats in the ballroom. I settled for a place in the back so that I could get an observer's eye-view of the proceedings. As the time for the opening session came near, you could feel the excitement mounting. Shirley's entrance was as well orchestrated as it might have been for one of her cabaret acts. Soon, there she was, bouncing effervescently onto the stage, looking considerably younger than her age, healthy, vibrant, and full of energy.

After a friendly bit of audience warm-up, we settled into a long day of lectures, question-and-answer sessions, and touchy-feely psychic exercises. If New Age thinking had been somewhat masked in her autobiographical exploits with lovers and her other superstar experiences, nothing was left uncovered in the New Age message being dished out here with Ms. MacLaine's typical flair and pizzazz. In fact, I was impressed with how conversant she was with her subject matter. The acid test of whether someone knows what they are talking about usually comes in question-and-answer sessions. Ms. MacLaine responded with poise, quick answers, and wide-ranging familiarity with New Age philosophy.

There was talk of "centering," "cosmic energy," "chakras," "healing crystals," and "consciousness raising." There were attempted demonstrations of aura sensing (which neither my hastily-matched partner and I nor our immediate neighbors were successful at achieving). But the shocker of the day came suddenly out of nowhere.

Having encouraged us to take responsibility for our own

lives, Ms. MacLaine turned directly to us and said matter-of-factly: "As Jesus and Buddha have said, 'Be still and know that *you* are God.'" The audience drank it in as a great revealed truth, unaware that neither Buddha nor Jesus had ever said that.

It seemed not to matter to either Ms. MacLaine or her audience that it was the Great Lie of the ages, dating all the way back to the Garden of Eden when Satan said to Eve, "You will be like God" (Genesis 3:5). If some of the lies being told by the New Age movement are subtle variations from the truth, this supreme lie is by no means subtle. It is a 180-degree twisting of the truth. In fact, it is a blasphemous reversal of Scripture which puts us in the place of God. "Be still and know that I am God," from Psalm 46:10, refers to the God of Creation, not to us. From the mouth of God, its message is plain and simple: God is God and, make no mistake about it, we are not.

In New Age thought, we are each the master of our own universe. We have infinite power over our circumstances, because, after all, we are God. But surely the best test of that belief is whether indeed we are able to control what happens to us. If there are ways in which we truly can take better control of our lives, can we *always* control our circumstances? And if we can't, is it simply because we have failed to fully appreciate that we are God?

What about the passengers who died on Pan Am flight #103? Did any of them have the power within themselves to prevent a bomb exploding at 21,000 feet? What about the people of Armenia who were trapped under tons of rubble from the earthquake? Must we attribute their inability to survive to their ignorance of New Age thought and the knowledge that they had the unlimited power of godhood? If they individually *were* God, why would they not have *known* that they were God, having the power of God?

And what about you and me? Do we, of ourselves, have the power to insure our safety when we bravely venture into the not-always-so-friendly skies? Or to stop the aging process? Or to prevent our own deaths? Can we, from the powers within the mind, restore sight from total blindness or heal a severed limb? Why is it that in times of crisis, virtually everyone (including New Agers) appeals to a greater power through such words as, "Oh, my God!" or "God help me"?

A time of crisis and helplessness is the context in which the psalmist refers to the words which were so blatantly abused by Ms. MacLaine.

God is our refuge and strength,
    an ever present help in trouble.
Therefore we will not fear, though the earth give way
    and the mountains fall into the heart of the sea,
though its waters roar and foam
    and the mountains quake with their surging.

"Be still, and know that I am God;
    I will be exalted among the nations,
I will be exalted in the earth."

The LORD Almighty is with us;
    the God of Jacob is our fortress. (Psalm 46:1-3; 10, 11)

When we have done all that we can do, there is One greater than ourselves to whom we can turn. When trouble comes our way, there is a God outside of ourselves who has unlimited power over every circumstance which might befall us. This is not to say that our unwavering belief in the God of Creation will heal every sickness, prevent inevitable death, or even relieve us of paying taxes. God does not promise to alleviate all of our problems, pain, or suffering. He *does* promise to be our strength when we find ourselves caught up in circumstances over which we have no control.

It's no good deluding ourselves that we are God when we

are not. The disappointing consequences of believing the Great Lie will come all too soon and with frustrating frequency. Like Adam and Eve who believed Satan in the Garden, we too *shall* surely die. We do not have the power over death. We are not God.

DECEPTION IN A GARDEN

But perhaps there was some confusion about what Shirley MacLaine was saying. Did she really intend to say that we are God? It wasn't long before Ms. MacLaine put us through an exercise intended to lead each of us to our "Higher Self." That was, after all, the purpose of the seminar—to get in touch with Higher Self. But who *was*, or what *is*, Higher Self?

The lights in the ballroom were lowered, and meditative wind chime music played on cue in the background. Closing our eyes as instructed, we listened while Ms. MacLaine talked us through a visualization sequence which, in abbreviated fashion, went something like this:

I want you to relax. Let every part of your body relax and feel free. Imagine yourself feeling lighter and lighter until you are actually floating. Float higher; now even higher. Feel the breeze as you begin to fly over the earth. ("Isn't this fun?" she interjected.) Imagine what the earth would look like as a tiny ball. Float above it, free and fluid. Now begin your descent. Come down, farther down. Come down slowly, slowly.

Look beneath you and you will see a lush green area. Let yourself down slowly into this garden of green until your bare feet are touching the cool mud. Let the mud ooze between your toes. Now look around you. You will see a path leading straight before you. Walk down the path. Reach out to the plants on either side of you along your way. Let them caress you.

Up ahead is a stream of cool, refreshing water, and a bridge across the stream. Walk onto the bridge and feel the coolness of the water beneath you. Reach out and feel the wet spray. Now look before you as the path leads on to a large opening in the garden. Walk slowly to that opening. There before you is a large tree, larger than any of the other trees.

Standing before you beneath the tree is the one you have come to seek. Let me introduce you to your Higher Self. Your Higher Self is the one to whom you have been praying. Your Higher Self is God!

The quietness of the room was penetrated by first one person, then another, softly crying. For many people, it obviously was a very moving experience. I opened my eyes and looked around with amazement, wondering how 800 people could be led so easily to the belief that the God to whom they had offered a lifetime of prayers was actually themselves.

It did not escape my attention that the Great Lie had been presented to the audience in the context of a garden and that the focal point of the lie was associated with a tree. Nothing has changed since the Great Lie was first told in the Garden of Eden regarding the forbidden fruit of the tree. Because a garden and a tree were successful the first time around, Satan must think he can use the same props over and over again with guaranteed success.

There was no longer any doubt about what Shirley had meant earlier in saying, "Be still and know that *you* are God." It was the culmination of her own experience when, with claimed reluctance, she first came to that realization herself. In *Out On a Limb,* Shirley was told by her friend and spiritual mentor, David, that she was God. In her television adaptation of that book, the scene is dramatized on the beach in Malibu near Shirley's home.

David tells Shirley that all the answers about life are within her, because she is God. When Shirley wonders aloud whether she might not become arrogant if she really believed she were God, David's response is one of reassurance. "Say to yourself that you are God," he tells Shirley. With only slight hesitation, she says quietly, "I am God." "No, louder," says David. "Say it louder." Once again, but louder, Shirley says, "I am God." Her words are still not said with sufficient conviction for David, so one last time he says, "Turn to the ocean and say it like you really mean it!" Obediently, Shirley turns to the ocean, stretches out her arms, and with full conviction shouts out, "I AM GOD!"

The camera holds tight on that scene, then fades away into a commercial break. It was a dramatic moment. It was *the* moment, because it was the central message of the book and of the film. It is also the central message of the New Age movement: I am God; you are God.

Among the many letters which I have received since writing *Out On a Broken Limb,* I have been told by some that they, too, have attended Ms. MacLaine's seminars. More than one person told me that Shirley's garden scenario had put them in touch with Christ, because it was Jesus whom they saw at the foot of the tree. It should not be difficult to anticipate that, for some, Jesus would be the imagined figure. Did not Shirley say that Higher Self was the one to whom we have been praying? For anyone with a Christian background, the figure of Christ will naturally be associated with higher power and prayer.

But not everyone in the audience saw so noble a figure at the foot of the tree. One writer (a disillusioned New Age hopeful) told me that what she saw was a hot dog! Perhaps she and I are soul mates, because what I saw would have been a good match for her image. As an observer, of course, I was less devoted to the exercise than others might have been. But at the moment Shirley introduced us to our Higher

Self, the first thing that popped into my mind was a loaf of Wonder Bread!

The punster inside me wanted to ask, "Does that mean that my Higher Self is *wonderful,* or that I am going to make a lot of *dough?*" A woman who heard me ask those facetious questions aloud during a television interview wrote me with sincere urgency, suggesting a rather deep interpretation of my Wonder Bread vision. "Jesus," she said, "is the bread of life and was described in Scripture as 'Wonderful.'" It was Jesus I saw as my Higher Self, she insisted. For her, even the balloons found on the Wonder Bread package should have had meaning for me. The red balloons represented Christ's blood. The blue represented blue sky, which, in turn, represented heaven. The white, containing all the colors in the spectrum of light, once again pointed to Jesus, the Light of the world. How could I possibly have missed such obvious symbolism, she rebuked me!

If people were being led to Jesus Christ as Lord and Savior, I could only praise Shirley MacLaine and other New Agers. But their view of Jesus as simply one among many enlightened spiritual guides and masters—no greater than Buddha—is far from the Jesus of the Bible. Their Jesus is nothing like the one and only Son of God, the Word made flesh, the Way, the Truth, and the Life—one of three persons in the triune godhead of the Bible. Their Jesus, who can be no greater than myself or yourself, is a God too small.

The real danger in imagining mental pictures of hot dogs and Wonder Bread is that we inevitably end up creating God in our own image. God can be anything or anyone we want God to be, even ourselves, if that is convenient. When God can be whatever we might imagine subjectively, we have no God at all—just a vivid imagination. Can we afford to rely on our imagination to give us strength in times of personal crisis? When helpless situations lead us to pray, is it to our own helplessness that we are to address self-directed prayers? Are we to believe that our Higher Self is no greater than our own *inadequacy?*

REDEFINING GOD

How can one possibly believe that he or she is God? It is happening with such frequency today that there must be *some* reason. It happens, first of all, through a redefinition of God. The traditional, biblical definition of a Creator God of the universe would not permit any of us to claim his status. We know that we did not create the universe in which we live. Indeed, we *could* not! But the New Age world view supplies us with a radically different scenario of God and creation.

In the New Age, God is no longer the personal God of the Bible, who interacts with man and works his will through history. Rather, God is an impersonal *god-force,* of which everything in the universe is a part. It is much the same as the "Star Wars" catch-phrase, "May the Force be with you."

In the New Age, as in much of Eastern mysticism and Greek philosophy, all is said to be one—whether matter, energy, or consciousness. The appropriate label is monism. And the resulting equation follows: all is one, God is one, we are one, therefore we are God. It's neat, it's clean, and it's sufficiently convincing for anyone who wants to believe it.

The New Age version of creation is somewhat more bizarre. In the beginning, so it is said, the *god-force* was a sleeping, slumbering, pulsating ball of energy. When it roused itself, it exploded, in Big Bang fashion, into billions and billions of individualized points of consciousness—each of which became a soul. These souls—all of which were God—found their way into the three-dimensional earth-plane and soon began to think of themselves as three-dimensional as well. (No clear explanation is given as to how the three-dimensional earth-plane itself came into existence.) When they began to think and act three-dimensionally, they forgot that they were God. Their Higher Selves became only lower selves—humans, with finite human thoughts.

The goal of the New Age, therefore, is to raise our

consciousness into realizing that who we really are is God: that we have been God from the very beginning and can be God once again if only we will acknowledge the illusion of our earthly existence. By admitting our godhood, we are able to transcend time and space and reconnect with the God that we are: infinite, cosmic, omnipotent.

Conceding that we can never achieve such a leap of logic, or even of faith, in one lifetime, our spiritual evolution is made possible through hundreds, if not thousands, of lifetimes. It is here that New Age thinking merges with yet another lie, the idea of reincarnation. Reincarnation becomes the change agent through which the soul is brought to the ultimate realization of its godhood.

More on reincarnation later. The important point here is that, by New Age thinking, there is no separation between each of us and God. God is not outside of ourselves. We are all part of a God force which has lost its way. But what does that leave us with? A God who could forget who he is? What kind of a God could that possibly be? Is this weak God a God that we would want even *ourselves* to be? If it is en-lightenment we seek, how can we turn to an entity that doesn't know who he, or it, really is?

Shirley MacLaine and other New Age proponents are not getting us in touch with Higher Self. Instead, they are degrading our lower selves to undifferentiated humanity lost in deception. They are dragging down any notion of divinity to the lowest common denominator, wherein God is not different from ourselves, or evil, or pollution, or even human waste! If all truly is one, then neither God nor man is greater than animals, plants, or the minutest of subatomic particles.

Is it not enough that we should have been created "in the image of God" (Genesis 1:27)? Have we not enough honor to have been singled out from among all creation as rulers over the earth (Genesis 1:28)? Must we fall once again from the precipice of pride, only to discover that we fell victim to the

Great Lie? It was the Creator of our universe who said, "Be still and know that I am God." Wishing it otherwise won't make it so. And given our need for strength to cope with circumstances over which we are powerless, who would even *want* to wish it so?

THREE

Christ or Christ-Consciousness?

T HE MINNEAPOLIS STUDIO AUDIENCE WAITED with anticipation as technicians readied the set for a local television talk show. I had been invited on the program to present a Christian perspective of the New Age movement along with Charles Silva who would be speaking on behalf of the movement. Silva, who represented himself as Shirley MacLaine's spiritual mentor, "David," in *Out On a Limb*, was in town to present his own seminar on New Age thought. His book, *Date with the Gods*, was a wildly fantastic collection of paranormal claims, centering around spaceships and an affair with an extraterrestrial girlfriend, supposedly from the galaxy of stars known as the Pleiades.

In his book, Silva claimed that while standing atop the Andes holding rocks in his hands, he was able to receive European radio broadcasts. That he had been able to materialize teddy bears into existence from out of thin air simply using his mental powers. That he had once been taken up into a spaceship and carried at great distances—even down into the depths of Lake Titicaca—before being released to the world as a special messenger of cosmic glad tidings to those of us on this planet.

Silva also claimed to have learned some amazing facts bearing on a wide variety of biblical occurrences. For example, he assures us that Adam and Eve, Earth's first two inhabitants, came to this planet from Venus. As for the destruction of Sodom and Gomorrah, Silva says it was an atom bomb that brought doom to those godless cities of old. Perhaps most revealing, Silva confirms that Jesus was indeed born of the virgin Mary, but it didn't happen quite like we have been led to believe. According to Silva, Mary was artificially inseminated by extraterrestrials using laser beams!

As you might imagine, Shirley MacLaine has gone to great lengths to distance herself from any connection with Charles Silva. However, his account of an affair with a girl from the Pleiades fits hand in glove with Ms. MacLaine's story of David and his girlfriend, Mayan, in *Out On a Limb*. In her book, Ms. MacLaine took at face value David's story that his cosmic information had come from a Pleiadian extra-terrestrial. And in the "green room" prior to the show, Silva revealed details of his association with Ms. MacLaine that convinced me he was at least one of the figures who made up the composite "David" character.

With all this in mind, later during the show I pointed out to the audience the chain of information on which millions of Shirley MacLaine followers were relying. "This man, Charles Silva, claims to have received his information from a woman coming to Earth from a distant galaxy," I began. "He, in turn, has given that information to Shirley MacLaine, who has shared it with millions of her readers, who have adopted its basic New Age message as their own personal statement of belief."

I assumed it would be obvious just how precarious that made any belief in New Age philosophy which might come by way of Shirley MacLaine. But as I looked out into the audience, imagine my surprise when the collective silent response obviously was, "*So?* What's so difficult to believe about that?" Despite the materialized teddy bears, virgin birth by laser beams, and claims of extraterrestrial origins for New Age insight, the audience didn't seem the least bit put off.

Are we to assume, then, that the audience was heavily weighted toward New Age supporters? I can tell you that virtually always, this has been the case whenever I have appeared on television talk shows to discuss the subject of New Age. New Age groupies seem to appear out of the woodwork. So it would not have been surprising if the audience for this show leaned toward New Age thinking. But the most interesting and insightful information about the audience, as well as the New Age movement in general, was revealed even before the show began.

During the audience warm-up, the host of the show wanted to get a feel for how many people in the audience were New Agers and how many were Christians. He first asked, "How many of you consider yourself to be a New Ager?" Of the 140 people in the studio audience, no less than 130 hands were raised. Then, thinking he would get the remaining ten studio guests to raise their hands, the host asked, "Okay, how many of you are Christians?" To both his and my own amazement, virtually every person in the audience raised a hand! The audience was indicating that they considered themselves to be *Christians* as well as New Agers!

ARE CHRISTIANITY AND NEW AGE COMPATIBLE?

In that moment was the most graphic confirmation possible of what I had been reading from many New Age sources: that New Age and Christian beliefs are compatible—at least that part of Christianity which New Agers are willing to accept, or to mold into conformity with New Age thought. Here, once again, we are confronted with another crystal lie. Virtually all of the major Christian themes, including sin, salvation, sacrificial atonement, grace, resurrection, judgment, heaven, and hell, are rejected outright by the New Age movement. But New Agers are undaunted. If they were brought up as Christians, Christians they will remain, even if they now believe a philosophy that runs completely counter to Christianity.

One of the fathers of the New Age movement, Edgar Cayce, was perhaps the first major proponent to blend together the teachings of Christ with the teachings of Eastern mysticism. Cayce, a Baptist Sunday school teacher, first gained notoriety from psychic healings. He later graduated to presenting "life readings," which claimed to give information regarding people's past lives. That supposed power did not manifest itself until Cayce did voluminous reading from among the scriptures of such Eastern religions as Hinduism and Buddhism.

Claiming cosmic insight into the person of Jesus Christ, Cayce says that Jesus incarnated, not once, but many times. According to Cayce, Jesus first incarnated as Adam, and, yes, did in fact commit the original sin (See Cayce's reading 2067-7). Jesus next incarnated as Enoch, the man who did not die but was taken up by God into heaven. A bit of a problem arises for Cayce at this point, since Adam and Enoch were living at the same time. But, for Cayce, it all works out in the end. In a later incarnation Jesus was Zend (the father of Zoroaster, founder of the Zoroastrian religion), whose own father was Uhjltd (Cayce himself in a prior incarnation). Cayce conveniently ends up being the father of the person whom we know as Jesus! That is about as far as a human being can go in reducing Jesus Christ to his own level.

But the outrageousness of Cayce's claims about Jesus' past lives or his own must not obscure the greater danger of the New Age message. We are being told that *each of us* can be Christ just as Jesus was Christ. We can be our own

Messiah. And, most important of all, we can become Lord of our own lives. In fact, we are told that Krishna and Buddha were Christs in their own right. In her book *Many Mansions*, Gina Cerminara, the chronicler of Edgar Cayce's readings, helps us make that breathtaking leap of insight:

> The Christ-consciousness is not, however, an exclusively Christian attribute. Christ, it must be remembered, is not the name of the man Jesus, but a term whose literal meaning is "the anointed one," and whose mystic or rather psychological meaning is that of the liberated or spiritual consciousness. Krishna and Buddha were, we may believe, equally the possessors of Christ-consciousness.

What's more, you and I can equally be the possessors of Christ-consciousness, we are told, when we open ourselves to an enlightened realization of who we really are.

And here, we come to both the heart of the New Age message and to the crux of its deception. New Age is the third of three mainline world views. The first, Christianity, is founded upon the belief that there is a Creator God of the universe who purposely created man as flesh and blood in a material environment, but also in God's own image spiritually; that man disobeyed the commands of God and was separated from God because of his sin; that reconciliation with God comes through faith in the atoning death of Jesus Christ on the cross.

The second perspective, secular humanism, assumes a mostly Darwinian view of the universe in which life came about through the chance process of Evolution. Consistent with that view, God is dead. There is no God. And man is simply at the top of the evolutionary chain of progression. Since there is no God and no spiritual aspect of man, then man has no need for reconciliation. There is no sin, no need for salvation, and certainly no need for a Savior.

For many decades now, secular humanism has been the belief of choice in secular society. It has held a tight grip in education, the media, and even politics. But it does not satisfy the hunger of the human soul. It is hopelessly materialistic. It is empty, and unfulfilling. Therefore, it is not surprising that many secular humanists find themselves searching for an alternative. That alternative is not likely to be pure Christianity, because for most humanists, the spiritual demands of Christianity are too great. Giving up the idea that man is supreme is too much to ask. But there has to be *some* dimension to man other than his being merely a highly evolved animal. There has to be *something* greater to believe in, *some* kind of transcendence.

That's where the New Age movement enters, being guaranteed instant success. For secular humanists, it must be like a breath of fresh air. Evolutionary origins are still honored, but somehow, someway, man is given a spiritual nature. And, achieving the best of both worlds, God is no longer dead—we *are* God! Naturally, it takes overcoming a wide chasm of rational belief in order to fully accept the fact that we are God, but that is the very bridge offered by the New Age movement. It is the leap of faith that Shirley MacLaine asks her followers to take in finding their Higher Selves.

In New Age thought, it is metaphysical ignorance that separates us from our own divinity. Ignorance, not sin, is the great moral failing of man. And the solution to ignorance is cosmic education, enlightened awareness. The clincher? Those who achieve that awareness and accept the fact that they really are God are no longer separated from true reality. They have overcome ignorance. They have bridged the gap between the material and the spiritual. And because they have become reconciled to themselves, they have achieved "Christ-consciousness." In short, they are their own Christ, their own Savior.

Therefore, if one wishes to think of himself as a Christian—

modeling himself after the reconciling ministry of Jesus of Nazareth—then he may do so with complete intellectual security. It hardly matters that he has driven yet another spike into the hands of Jesus on the cross, who died so that one who turns to Christ will be forgiven of his sins. It hardly matters that he has blasphemously put himself in the place of the true Messiah. It seems to be of no consequence that he has deceived himself into thinking he is one and the same as the sinless Son of God who was born miraculously of the virgin Mary. In the New Age, if a person wishes to become his own God and Savior, he can still think of himself as a Christian.

TRADITIONAL CHRISTIAN CULTS

The marriage of East and West, of Christianity and paganism, took place long before the New Age movement came on the scene. In fact it has been institutionalized for many years in the form of numerous Christian cults. Among those who would call themselves Christians or who would honor Christ in the religious labels which they wear are millions of people who believe and practice what is, in effect, Eastern mysticism.

Madame Blavatsky's Theosophy, begun in the late 1800s, is heavily weighted toward the spiritism of the East. Her book, *Isis Unveiled,* taught the soul's capacity to become God through inner enlightenment. Out of that school of thought came Alice Bailey, who is credited with first giving the New Age movement its name. The tie with Christianity is obvious from the title of her 1948 book, *Reappearance of the Christ.*

In the tradition of neopagan, metaphysical, and spiritualist churches come also the Church of Religious Science, the Church of Divine Science, and the Unitarians Universalist Church. While ties with the New Age movement would be stoutly rejected, the thread also winds its way to

Christian Science (the Church of Christ, Scientist). Its denial of evil and of the essential existence of a material world, together with healing through the mind, fit particularly well with New Age teaching. Nor can one overlook Mormonism (The Church of Jesus Christ of Latter Day Saints), in which the believer is on his way to becoming a god, or even Jehovah's Witnesses, who claim that Jesus was only a son of God, which we all can become in an equal sense.

Let me stress again that most of these churches would have no part of the New Age movement itself, but they unquestionably drink from the same fountain in many of their more significant doctrinal beliefs. Christianity has been compromised repeatedly throughout the centuries with ties to metaphysical and mystical beliefs. Indeed, even in the first century, metaphysical Gnosticism worked its way into the early Christian church.

The attempt of the New Age movement to find compatibility with Christianity is building on well-laid foundations. Hardly anything about the New Age movement is really new, except perhaps for its Westernized, glitzy packaging.

When you think about it, there are only a limited number of responses to the issue of God and man. Man can think of God as a personal, involved God of revelation and history (theism), or as a detached, disinterested God (deism), or as an immaterial force throughout nature (animism), or as an idol (paganism); or as non-existent altogether (atheism).

The New Age movement contains elements of all of the above. It attempts to incorporate the revealed teaching of Jesus Christ (theism), but disclaims a God working his purpose throughout history (deism), affirming instead that all is one (animism), and that we find power in crystals, yoga, and tarot cards (paganism), but that the bottom line is that there is no God outside of ourselves (atheism). To all of that the New Age movement adds heaping bowlfuls of self-worship (Me-ism).

In such an equation, the Christ of Christianity loses out. In fact, not even Hinduism or Buddhism, which are held in such high esteem by New Agers, emerge unscathed. New Age is not the best of all worlds, but the worst. It lacks coherence, defies consistency, and demeans altogether the notion of divinity.

JESUS—EVERYONE WANTS HIM

Like seemingly everyone else, New Agers *want* to believe in Jesus. They want him on their team. They know that without Jesus, the game can't begin. Even when New Agers refer to Jesus and Buddha in the same breath, as if they were on a spiritual par, invariably it is Jesus whom they will quote, not Buddha. They know that it is not Buddha with whom they must deal, but Jesus. Try as they might to equate the two, Jesus will have none of it. He claims exclusivity. He, and only he, shows us the way to God. He, and only he, exercised the power of God. He, and only he, *is* God.

> Jesus answered, "I am the way and the truth and the life. No one comes to the Father except through me. (John 14:6)

Jesus was not just a wonderful teacher and ascended Master. He cannot be put on the same level as Buddha, Krishna, Mohammed, or enlightened yogis. Which of them calmed the storm-tossed waves? Which of them healed the sick of their diseases? Or turned water into wine, or fed 5000 people with a few loaves and fishes? Or drove out demons, or raised people from the dead? Which of them raised *himself* from the dead? Jesus did what no one else in all of recorded history has been able to do. Jesus alone was God incarnate!

DID JESUS TEACH THE DEITY OF HUMANKIND?

New Agers cite to us a statement by Jesus that says, as they interpret it, we too shall be as gods:

> Jesus answered them, "Is it not written in your Law, 'I have said you are gods?'" (John 10:34)

Both the context and its Old Testament antecedent are ignored. In the following passage, look closely at the context and the significance of Jesus' claim to be God. It was this very claim that brought about anger against his apparent blasphemy (blasphemy only if he was *not* God, as he claimed to be!).

> "I and the Father are one."
> Again the Jews picked up stones to stone him, but Jesus said to them, "I have shown you many great miracles from the Father. For which of these do you stone me?"
> "We are not stoning you for any of these," replied the Jews, "but for blasphemy, because you, a mere man, claim to be God."
> Jesus answered them, "Is it not written in your Law, 'I have said you are gods?' If he called them 'gods,' to whom the word of God came—and the Scripture cannot be broken—what about the one whom the Father set apart as his very own and sent into the world? Why then do you accuse me of blasphemy because I said, 'I am God's Son?' Do not believe me unless I do what my Father does. But if I do it, even though you do not believe me, believe the miracles, that you may know and understand that the Father is in me, and I in the Father." (John 10:30-38)

The first thing we must recognize is that Jesus was not teaching New Age monism (that all is one and God is one, so we are God). When he said that he and the Father were one, he underscored the fact that the Father had *set him apart* as his very own. The Jews correctly appreciated that Jesus was not including everyone in the oneness of the godhood. To the contrary, Jesus was singling himself out as *exclusively* one with God.

Secondly, Jesus was not saying that each of us is a god. He is quoting Psalm 82, which refers to the judges of Israel as "gods" when they dispense justice as God's agents on earth. In their case, the judges were reminded that their failure to properly dispense justice would cause them to die like the mere men they were.

> God presides in the great assembly;
>   he gives judgment among the "gods":
> "How long will you defend the unjust
>   and show partiality to the wicked?
> Defend the cause of the weak and fatherless;
>   maintain the rights of the poor and oppressed.
> Rescue the weak and needy;
>   deliver them from the hand of the wicked.
> They know nothing, they understand nothing.
>   They walk about in darkness;
>   all the foundations of the earth are shaken.
> I said, 'You are "gods";
>   you are all sons of the Most High.'
> But you will die like mere men;
>   you will fall like every other ruler."
> Rise up, O God, judge the earth,
>   for all the nations are your inheritance. (Psalm 82)

In referring to this psalm and the phrase "You are 'gods,'" Jesus was leading the Jews back to his own exclusive identity. Judges may be "gods" in the sense that they might act on God's behalf, but Jesus was claiming much more than that. He was claiming to be the only begotten son of God, God made flesh, God sent into the world to claim sinners.

In the prologue to his gospel account, the apostle John made clear this distinction:

> In the beginning was the Word, and the Word was with God, and the Word was God. He was with God in the beginning.
> Through him all things were made; without him nothing was made that has been made. In him was life, and that life was the light of men.
> The Word became flesh and lived for a while among us.We have seen his glory, the glory of the one and only Son, who came from the Father, full of grace and truth. (John 1:1-4, 14)

Jesus, the Word made flesh, was in the beginning with God, and—more importantly—*was* God. He was the God who created the world. The God in whom there is life. The "One and Only" God.

The apostle Paul also testifies to the unique nature of Jesus Christ.

> He is the image of the invisible God, the firstborn over all creation. For by him all things were created: things in heaven and on earth, visible and invisible, whether thrones or powers or rulers or authorities; all things were created by him and for him. He is before all things, and in him all things hold together. And he is the head of the body, the church; he is the beginning and the firstborn from among the dead, so that in everything he might have the supremacy. For God was pleased to have all his fullness dwell in him, and through him to reconcile to himself all things, whether things on earth or things in heaven, by making peace through his blood, shed on the cross. (Colossians 1:15-20)

The broken Christ, hanging limp on the cross, does not square with New Age teaching, which says that we have the power within us to overcome every circumstance. For our sake, the Son of God yielded his divine power in order to become subject to the cruelty of the cross. In that supreme act of love and mercy, there was no power of positive thinking. No human potential. No fire-walking, spoon-bending, mind-over-matter psychokinesis. No holistic healing. No astral projections. No consciousnessraising or chakra cleansing. Just human suffering and the same death that you and I one day will experience.

But the story of Jesus does not end with his death. To the people of ancient Athens, most of whom would feel completely comfortable with today's New Age movement, the apostle Paul brought a reminder of two aspects of Christianity which are denied by "New Age Christians"— resurrection and final judgment:

> In the past God overlooked such ignorance, but now he commands all people everywhere to repent. For he has set a day when he will judge the world with justice by the man he has appointed. He has given proof of this to all men by raising him from the dead. (Acts 17:30, 31)

It is our faith in the resurrection of Christ that gives us hope for our own life after death. The New Age movement has succeeded only in emptying the gospel of Christ of its power. In its blatant deception about the true nature of Jesus Christ, it has marked itself as antichrist:

> Who is the liar? It is the man who denies that Jesus is the Christ. Such a man is the antichrist—he denies the Father and the Son. No one who denies the Son has the Father; whoever acknowledges the Son has the Father also. (1 John 2:22, 23)

The New Age movement: enlightened Christianity or deceptive antichrist? The stakes are high. Nothing less than eternal life is at risk.

FOUR

The Global Gossip Game

H AVE YOU EVER WONDERED where we got all the different
religions of the world? Why do billions of the earth's
inhabitants worship in radically different ways? What
explains the variety of major world religions? Perhaps more
intriguing, what explains their common threads of brotherhood, love, and morality? What in man causes him to
worship, and to believe in a life after death?

Perhaps the answers to all these questions are found in
the Global Gossip Game. Remember the game of "Gossip"
that we used to play at parties? (I think a more up-to-date
generation may call it the "Telephone" game.)The first
person tells something to the second person who, in turn,
tells it to the next person. As the message quickly goes from
person to person around the room, it keeps changing ever so
slightly. By the time it gets to the last person, it only faintly
resembles what the first person said. That's why it is so
appropriately named the "Gossip" game. Gossip has a nasty
way of distorting the truth.

A similar process of skewed communication may account
for much of the diversity among world religions. It may also
explain why, despite the differences, there are common
threads of belief among all religions. If they all came from the
same original source, it should not be surprising that they

would share certain uniform concerns.

Many early writings refer to the creation of the world or to various creation myths: The most detailed account, presented as historical fact, is contained in the Bible, in the Book of Genesis. If we assume the validity of the Genesis account and its record of mankind's beginning, we immediately are faced with three mind-boggling facts. First, that the entire universe, as vast and complex as it is, was brought into existence by a being so powerful and intelligent that we can hardly even imagine his infinite nature. Second, that he chose to create us in some way like himself. And third, that he desires relationship with us. So much so, in fact, that he dared to communicate directly with the first human beings, Adam and Eve.

All of that is simply too glib to match the reality of what actually happened. It glosses over billions upon billions of creation details, and the wonder of God literally talking to men and women, his highest creation. How did he do that? What language did he use? More important—*why* did he do that? Why would the God of all creation seek a relationship with men and women made of dust?

Without being privy to all the details, if we accept the fact of its occurrence, then the Global Gossip Game has begun. Communicating directly with Adam and Eve, God gave guidelines for their meaningful existence in the Garden. As we know, they disobeyed those guidelines and were sent out of the Garden into the world of sin and death which they had created through their disobedience.

FROM FAITHFULNESS TO REJECTION

Soon we find that God is communicating with the children of Adam and Eve. For example, we see God talking directly with Cain, who had offered a displeasing sacrifice to God.

Then the LORD said to Cain, "Why are you angry? Why is your face downcast? If you do what is right, will you not be accepted? But if you do not do what is right, sin is crouching at your door; it desires to have you, but you must master it." (Genesis 4:6, 7)

Whatever else God may have said to Adam and Eve and to their children, he clearly told them what was right and what was wrong. Already Cain had done something wrong, and he was about to do something else tragically wrong. Killing his brother Abel in jealous anger would result in his being banished to live in the land of Nod, east of Eden.

It is important to note that by this time—apparently many decades since creation—the family of man already had begun to multiply rapidly. Presumably the offspring resulted from marriages among the sons and daughters of Adam and Eve. And they had already begun to spread to great distances, as indicated by Cain's response to his punishment for killing Abel:

Cain said to the LORD, "My punishment is more than I can bear. Today you are driving me from the land, and I will be hidden from your presence; I will be a restless wanderer on the earth, and whoever finds me will kill me." (Genesis 4:13, 14)

Two more interesting pieces of the puzzle fall into place at this point. After the birth of Seth, the Genesis record says succinctly: "At that time men began to call on the name of the LORD" (Genesis 4:26). Yet within seven generations, "The LORD saw how great man's wickedness on the earth had become, and that every inclination of the thoughts of his heart was only evil all the time" (Genesis 6:5). Man had the capacity for good and for evil. If there were times when he worshipped the God of creation, there were other times when he did not. If there were some men and women who bowed their heads to God, others did not.

Already the message was going awry in the Global Gossip Game. In fact, it had gone so far off track that God repented of having ever made man and of having sought a relationship with him. But in the righteousness of Noah and his family, there was yet a glimmer of hope. After the Flood, which God sent as a means of calling mankind back to the original message of his truth, Noah and his descendants repopulated the earth: "These were the three sons of Noah, and from them came the people who were scattered over the earth" (Genesis 9:19).

If the three sons of Adam and Eve could have different views about God and how to worship him, it should not be surprising that the three sons of Noah and their descendants could also develop significantly different religious outlooks in the centuries to follow.

THE SPREAD OF CULTURE

What happened next is an important key both to the Global Gossip Game and to an understanding of the New Age movement. Somewhere around 2000 B.C., we find mankind turning the focus away from God and toward themselves. It was not just a matter of individual men and women rejecting God. It was a *movement*. In fact, it was the first recorded human potential movement. And it had gained momentum because of the ease of communication. At that time, there was still only one language among those who inhabited the earth.

Language, culture, and religion typically go hand in hand. But words that had once taught of submission to the one God, the Creator of the universe, were now being used to claim that man no longer needed God; that, with impunity, man could do whatever he wanted to do; that he could create his own reality; that he himself could be God. Not surprisingly, the results brought a swift response from God. The Book of Genesis records for us the events of this spiritual and linguistic watershed in man's history:

> Now the whole world had one language and a common speech. As men moved eastward, they found a plain in Shinar and settled there.
>
> They said to each other, "Come, let's make bricks and bake them thoroughly." They used brick instead of stone, and tar for mortar. Then they said, "Come, let us build ourselves a city, with a tower that reaches to the heavens, so that we may make a name for ourselves and not be scattered over the face of the whole earth."
>
> But the LORD came down to see the city and the tower that the men were building. The LORD said, "If as one people speaking the same language they have begun to do this, then nothing they plan to do will be impossible for them. Come, let us go down and confuse their language so they will not understand each other."
>
> So the LORD scattered them from there over all the earth, and they stopped building the city. That is why it was called Babel—because there the LORD confused the language of the whole world. From there the LORD scattered them over the face of the whole earth. (Genesis 11:1-9)

Three significant observations must be made about this amazing episode in the history of man. First, differences in language will point the way to differences in religion and culture. Even with a common language, the "gossip" about God had already become confused. Now, that confusion would only increase.

Second, global dispersion of the population meant that, as with all other communication, dialogue about God would increasingly diminish. Diverse cultures and civilizations, together with their ideas about God, would become more and more isolated from each other. Whatever view a given culture adopted would become entrenched, solidified, and highly refined. If common threads of belief survived in each evolving form, the acquired differences would tend to dominate the expression of those common beliefs.

Third, the events of Babel pointed the direction in which major world religions would tend to go. Whenever religious belief was allowed to stray from perceiving God as the God of creation, who seeks a personal relationship with man through direct communication of his purpose and will, the tendency would be to view God as some part of creation itself. Something in the universe would be elevated to the level of deity, whether it were a sun god or moon god; a piece of wood or molten image worshiped as an idol; a more encompassing, intangible force found throughout all of nature; or man himself, the highest of God's creation and the supreme object of idolatry.

As we have already suggested, the New Age movement incorporates each of these elements of pagan worship into its belief system. Its environmental concern is not based upon the role God has given man to rule the earth wisely and with stewardship, but upon a cult-like devotion to Mother Earth, as a source of energy and life. Even the stars and other planets are worshiped through current New Age fascination with astrology and horoscopes. And wooden idols and golden calves have merely been replaced by quartz crystals. You find them set up as twentieth century altars in the back rooms of New Age bookstores and in living rooms of New Agers across the land.

The view of God as a force found throughout nature is adopted by New Agers in its updated versions of monism and pantheism. The God of both heaven and history loses his personhood to an impersonal energy force void of relationship or communication. And man once again becomes the object of veneration as he himself becomes God. In one fell swoop, the New Age movement has managed to deceive us in every way possible about the true nature of God. Instead of man's being made in the image of God, in the New Age movement, God is made in the image of man.

THE MAJOR RELIGIONS

When I was just a boy, I thought that the only people in the world of the Old Testament were the people of Israel or, at most, those other nations with whom the Israelites came into contact. It never occurred to me that there were people in India, China, or South America during the centuries before Christ. Of course, more mature understanding brought me to realize that after the incident at Babel and God's dispersion of the people, the Bible narrows its focus to God's chosen nation of Israel. The Genesis record falls mostly silent upon the earth's inhabitants except for the descendants of Shem, down to Abraham, the father of the Hebrews. It would be through the Hebrew nation that God would ultimately speak in a new way to the whole world, in the person of Jesus the Christ. Therefore, the Old Testament is devoted almost entirely to the Hebrews, the nation of Israel whose people became known as Jews.

After centuries of on-again off-again allegiance to God, the Jews eventually fell victim to the arrogance of being God's special people. Focusing on themselves rather than God, they forgot God. And when they forgot God, they turned to the worship of idols—creatures of their own making—just like the nations around them. Post-exilic Judaism became an institutionalized attempt at pleasing the God of heaven, but never recaptured the religious fervor of its faithful forebears.

Because of their intertwined histories, we know somewhat of the idolatry practiced by Israel's neighbors, Egypt and Persia. But far off in distant lands the Global Gossip Game was taking some unusual twists. In India, as early as

1500 B.C., a complex form of idolatry was developing. Moving from the one sovereign God of creation to a polytheistic religion of many gods, Hinduism eventually changed the definition of God altogether. No longer was there an external God actively working through history on behalf of his people. By Hindu thought, nothing existed apart from true self, which was part of an all-encompassing cosmic energy force.

In Hinduism, the personal God of creation was replaced by the impersonal law of karma. Karma is a law of cause and effect which dictates one's position in life, depending upon one's conduct. While the Law of Moses was laying a foundation for human equality, the law of karma was trapping people into rigid social groupings known as castes. A person's caste was determined according to his or her karma. Good karma put you into the highest level of society, the Brahman caste. Bad karma found you on the lowest rung of the ladder, as a degraded "untouchable."

The most remarkable feature of Hinduism was its concept of the afterlife. Although biblical Judaism was only slowly developing its definition of what happens to man after death, it was taken for granted that each person had only one lifetime. In one of their psalms, the sons of Korah ask rhetorically, "Do those who are dead rise up and praise you?" (Psalm 88:10). In his wise sayings, Agur asks, "Who has gone up to heaven and come down? . . . Tell me if you know!" (Proverbs 30:4).

When contemplating his death, King Hezekiah of Judah laments, "I will not again see the LORD, the Lord, in the land of the living; no longer will I look on mankind, or be with those who now dwell in this world" (Isaiah 38:11). And King Solomon answers the question of whether the dead will return to the earth, saying, "Never again will they have a part in anything that happens under the sun" (Ecclesiastes 9:6).

In Hinduism, by contrast, life is believed to be cyclical.

Through the process of reincarnation, each person lives many lifetimes on the earth. In fact, it is an endless cycle of transmigration, in which the soul may even devolve into a non-human form, such as a rock, a frog, or a tree. The form of one's re-entry into the physical universe is determined, once again, by the law of karma.

Some 500 years before Christ, a Hindu monk named Siddhartha Gautama, defiant of the "infernal wheel of reincarnation," devised a system of disciplined living aimed at breaking the cycle of death, birth, and rebirth which inevitably led to human suffering. He taught that through enlightenment, one could free himself from the illusions of the material world and achieve nirvana—eternal bliss. As the great teacher of enlightenment, he became known as the Buddha, "the Enlightened One." Hence the origin of Buddhism, which, together with Hinduism, lend much to the philosophical presuppositions of the New Age movement.

In many ways similar to Hinduism and Buddhism, other Eastern religions became creature-oriented, mystical, and spiritist. In China, Confucianism was the ethical system developed by Confucius (551-479 B.C.). This system of belief emphasized the development of social order through formal education and etiquette. Devotion to family, including ancestral spirits (more commonly known as ancestor worship), once again focused on human beings—creatures—rather than the Creator.

China's more mystical contribution to religious thought, Taoism, was founded by "the old master," Lao-tze, as early as the sixth century B.C. Lao-tze taught the concept of the Tao—"the way"—which was an impersonal concept of ultimate reality. Lao-tze's Tao saw all of life as cyclical, much like Hinduism's life and death cycle. From day and night, to seasons and years, to wet and dry, nature followed observable patterns. The key to successful living, therefore, is to place one's own life into harmony with these patterned forces of nature. One's life should be a simple honest life, particularly avoiding any interference with the course of natural events. Failure to harmonize with nature brings inevitable failure, disease, even death.

Central to the teaching of Taoism is the duality of life as expressed in *yin* (passivity) and *yang* (activity). Perhaps you have seen the ancient symbol of T'ai-chi T'u, the "diagram of the supreme ultimate," which is a circle divided in half by a curved line, leaving each half to look like a tear drop. The left half is white, except for a small black "eye" in its widest part which is at the top of the circle; the right half is black, except for a small white "eye" in its widest part which is at the bottom of the circle. The idea of the diagram is to express the interplay of *yin* and *yang* as the fundamental forces of nature.

In Taoism, all opposites are seen as two sides of the same coin. Light and dark, hot and cold, top and bottom, masculine and feminine, life and death are all part of a harmonious unity in nature. Therefore even good and evil are without ultimate distinction. The key to living is found in balance, centering, and harmony with nature. The forces of Nature become truth. Nature itself becomes man's judge. If you get out of line with nature, it will bring about natural disaster.

Taoism laid an early foundation for Zen (meaning meditation), a Japanese school of twelfth century Chinese origin. In Zen, the contemplation of one's essential nature to the exclusion of all else is the only way to achieve pure enlightenment.

Japan's Shinto religion is more polytheistic, even allowing for the Emperor worship which we have witnessed in this century with the deification of the late Emperor Hirohito. Until Japan's defeat at the hands of the United States in World War II, Hirohito was regarded as God incarnate and high priest of the Shinto faith.

Whether it was the nature worship of Taoism, ancestor worship of Confucianism, the mystical god-force of

Hinduism and Buddhism—when the Global Gossip Game had run its course, the personal, active, involved Creator God of history was set aside in favor of lesser gods and human philosophy.

THE PRICE OF PAGANISM

Centuries after the development of the world's other major religions, the apostle Paul would describe the deception offered by the false religions of the world:

> The wrath of God is being revealed from heaven against all the godlessness and wickedness of men who suppress the truth by their wickedness, since what may be known about God is plain to them, because God has made it plain to them. For since the creation of the world God's invisible qualities—his eternal power and divine nature—have been clearly seen, being understood from what has been made, so that men are without excuse. (Romans 1:18-20)

For Paul, the creation itself is witness to the one true God. Only a man or woman suffering the delusion of human pride can look about the universe and attribute its existence to his or her own power or to some other force within the universe itself. The psalmist expressed it well: "The fool says in his heart, 'There is no God'" (Psalm 14:1).

It is the arrogance of those who claim to be enlightened that is their ultimate undoing. It blinds them to truth. It welcomes deception with open arms.

> For although they knew God, they neither glorified him as God nor gave thanks to him, but their thinking became futile and their foolish hearts were darkened. Although they claimed to be wise, they became fools and

exchanged the glory of the immortal God for images made to look like mortal man and birds and animals and reptiles. (Romans 1:21-23)

No wonder that crystal lies are so easily accepted in the New Age movement. Trusting in self-validating intuition, all thinking has become futile. New Agers have exchanged the truth about a personal, omnipotent, caring God for an impersonal, finite, and uncaring god-force created in their own imagination.

What we believe is not merely academic. Not all religions are the same. Not all beliefs lead to the same end. Paul saw the kind of people we can become when we take our eyes off the true God:

Therefore God gave them over in the sinful desires of their hearts to sexual impurity for the degrading of their bodies with one another. They exchanged the truth of God for a lie, and worshiped and served created things rather than the Creator—who is forever praised. Amen. (Romans 1:24-25)

Morality suffers a death blow when we worship ourselves as God. In Chapter 8 we will see just how bankrupt the moral standards of the New Age movement have become.

Yet before we dismiss altogether the influence of major world religions, we must not forget their common roots. Basic morality, general principles of right and wrong, and common notions of fair play would educate the consciences of those within each religion. It is no secret why virtually all religions give honor to love, peace, and the brotherhood of man. If ritual were distorted, if a proper image of God were blurred by misunderstanding, if human error twisted ultimate reality into incorrect perceptions of man's duty before God, there would always be the haunting reality of the true God in whose image man was made. And despite its varied wrappings, the basic package requires a minimal standard of human conduct that is expected in virtually every culture and religion which has ever existed.

God and his divine moral order cannot be set aside by even the most outrageous gossip! Nor can God's judgment, which will be directed to every individual who ever lived, regardless of culture or religion:

> (Indeed, when Gentiles, who do not have the law, do by nature things required by the law, they are a law for themselves, even though they do not have the law, since they show that the requirements of the law are written on their hearts, their consciences also bearing witness, and their thoughts now accusing, now even defending them.) This will take place on the day when God will judge men's secrets through Jesus Christ, as my gospel declares. (Romans 2:14-16)

When God created man in his own image, he created him with moral conscience—a rational sense of personal accountability corresponding with the moral laws which undergird the physical universe. When man chooses to dull his conscience to the moral rule of God, he subjects himself to the wrath of the Creator who instilled that sense of right and wrong within him.

Once again we come to the fork in the road. Will we honor God as our Creator or ourselves who are mere creatures on this planet? Will we presume to have power over our circumstances that we cannot possibly have, or will we develop to their optimum the abilities which God has given us, and then place our trust in his power to achieve our potential?

It's not just a matter of power politics—whether *we* are God or *God* is God. It's a matter of preventing our own self-deception. Real power lies in truth. Ideas masquerading as truth can only limit us.

FIVE

At The Extremes of Belief

I NTO THE GLOOM OF DEVELOPING WORLD RELIGIONS in which
man had turned from the God of creation to powerless
lesser gods and impotent mystical philosophies came the
most mind-boggling possibility of all. God came into the
world in human flesh in the person of Jesus of Nazareth. God
broke into our universe, into our own finite dimension, so
that we could overcome the enemy of death. "For God so
loved the world that he gave his one and only Son, that
whoever believes in him shall not perish but have eternal
life" (John 3:16).

Conceived miraculously in the womb of a virgin, fulfilling
centuries of prophecy in the minutest detail, performing
miracles that no person before or since has been able to
demonstrate, demanding the very highest standard of
human actions and motives, demonstrating in his own life
the purity and love which he taught, dying for his claims to
be God in the flesh, and bringing hope to all mankind
through his own resurrection from the dead, Jesus turned
religion on its ear.

Even the Jewish leaders of his day, who believed in the
one God of heaven, were embarrassed by his call for a
religion, not of rituals and rules, but of compassion, justice,
and righteous living. And being disappointed that he had

not come as a political or military savior, as they had envisioned the promised Messiah, they rejected his spiritual kingship. In a sense, they too had abandoned the living God for a dead system of religious law of man's own making. In their devotion to man-made law, they had risked becoming as idolatrous as those who carved wooden idols, or worshiped the sun, or reduced God to an intangible force of nature.

To the secular humanist, Jesus taught the spiritual essence of man—his soul. To the metaphysicist, he affirmed the existence of physical matter and man's humanity—his body. To each came his warning that man faces the judgment of God as to which world view he chooses to follow: "Do not be afraid of those who kill the body but cannot kill the soul. Rather, be afraid of the one who can destroy both soul and body in hell" (Matthew 10:28).

The gospel of Christ was a balance of the physical and the spiritual. If in his model prayer (Matthew 6:9-13) Jesus gave priority to the coming of his spiritual kingdom into the physical universe, he also recognized the importance of one's daily bread to sustain the body while seeking a spiritual relationship with God.

His very presence on earth affirmed God's caring involvement in our lives. In the person of Jesus, God affirmed that he was not just some impersonal energy force or some distant, detached, deistic god.

> Therefore, since we have a great high priest who has gone through the heavens, Jesus the Son of God, let us hold firmly to the faith we profess. For we do not have a high priest who is unable to sympathize with our weaknesses, but we have one who has been tempted in every way, just as we are—yet was without sin. Let us then approach the throne of grace with confidence, so that we may receive mercy and find grace to help us in our time of need. (Hebrews 4:14-16)

Through his willingness to become weak on our behalf, we gain access to true universal power—the power of God working in us and through us. Where human potential inevitably ends at our own doorstep, faith in Jesus brings us into partnership with God. *Our* burdens become *his* burdens. *Our* weaknesses invite *his* strength.

> "Come to me, all you who are weary and burdened, and I will give you rest. Take my yoke upon you and learn from me, for I am gentle and humble in heart, and you will find rest for your souls. For my yoke is easy and my burden is light." (Matthew 11:28-30)

Jesus' teaching was not the skewed message of a Global Gossip Game gone amok. He brought religion back to the truth of God's exclusive divinity. He challenged man to become all that being made in God's image was meant to be but cautioned that God is God and we are not. He challenged man to look beyond materialism, and even vain religious exercise, to man's own spiritual self. And he condemned authoritarian, tradition-bound, empty religious expression. If organized Christianity later would be the victim of its own misguided doctrinal gossip game, Jesus and his teaching had captured the attention of millions of true seekers.

THE THREAT OF GNOSTICISM

Even before the first century of Christianity came to an end, it was threatened by a mystical world view known as Gnosticism. The literal meaning of *gnosis* is related to our word *knowledge*. It was taken as the catch-word for "those in the know." As modern-day descendants of the Gnostics, New Agers claim to be the ones who are "in the know," the truly enlightened ones. Like New Agers, the ancient

Gnostics of Greek and Roman culture believed that man is destined for reunion with the divine essence from which each soul has come.

Also like New Agers, the Gnostics denied the ultimate reality of matter. And because to them the body did not really exist, they convinced themselves that they could do in the body whatever they wished. They could even be immoral if they wanted. Only the spirit really counted, and it was separate from the body. Not surprisingly, the Gnostics lapsed into wholesale immorality, all the while claiming superior spiritual insight and enlightenment.

Both the apostle Peter, in his second epistle, and Jude, in his brief letter written about A.D. 60-80, confront a group of Gnostics who were claiming to be Christians, despite the obvious conflict in world views. In fact, they were teaching Gnosticism right alongside Christianity, as if the two beliefs were wholly compatible.

The similarity of the New Age movement with first century "Christian Gnosticism" (itself an oxymoron) warrants a close look at Jude's letter, which warns against such a dangerous heresy. Jude saw the "New Age movement" of his day to be a direct threat to Christian faith:

> Dear friends, although I was very eager to write to you about the salvation we share, I felt I had to write and urge you to contend for the faith that was once for all entrusted to the saints. For certain men whose condemnation was written about long ago have secretly slipped in among you. They are godless men, who change the grace of our God into a license for immorality and deny Jesus Christ our only Sovereign and Lord. (Jude 3, 4)

In the New Age movement, the most surprising thing is that no one seems to be the least bit interested in having the gift of God's grace. *Accepting* God's grace tacitly admits that we have sinned, that we are subject to spiritual condemnation, and that we need forgiveness through a power greater than ourselves. None of these assumptions are popular in the New Age. According to New Age thought, there is no God outside of ourselves against whom we can sin, there is no Judgment Day, and therefore no need for forgiveness by God's grace.

Such a perspective of man's inability to sin naturally opens the door to immoral conduct. The New Age movement is notorious for throwing out all objective standards of right and wrong, and its record on morality is predictably dismal.

We have already noted that Jesus is regarded by the New Age movement as a great master and teacher, but certainly not as the one and only Son of God. Like the Gnostics, who wanted to include Jesus within their mystical package—as if to give it credibility—New Agers deny that Jesus Christ is "our only Sovereign and Lord." For them, there is no sovereign, no Lord, outside of ourselves. We are the masters of our fate. We are in control.

Jude well knew that such a blasphemous world view cannot be ignored by a God who has said, "You shall have no other gods before me" (Deuteronomy 5:7). New Agers, like the Gnostics of Jude's day, have the ignominious distinction of being identified with disobedient fallen angels and the wicked people of Sodom and Gomorrah:

> Though you already know all this, I want to remind you that the Lord delivered his people out of Egypt, but later destroyed those who did not believe. And the angels who did not keep their positions of authority but abandoned their own home—these he has kept in darkness, bound with everlasting chains for judgment on the great Day. In a similar way, Sodom and Gomorrah and the surrounding towns gave themselves up to sexual immorality and perversion. They serve as an example of those who suffer the punishment of eternal fire. (Jude 5-7)

Denying a God of judgment is certainly an option. We can choose to believe that there is no judgment to face when we die. But if Jude is right and we are wrong, then we are taking a great risk. Certainly no one wants to conduct his life pursuant to the threat of punishment, but neither can the possibility easily be ignored. Indeed, if Jude is right about the rebellious angels and the people of Sodom and Gomorrah, then the possibility of punishment is real.

NEW AGE GNOSTICISM

Jude's description of the "Gnostic Christians" is striking in its similarity to New Agers. Throughout the text, let me insert some of the obvious parallels.

In the very same way, these dreamers pollute their own bodies [*through mind-altering drugs which some New Agers have advocated in the pursuit of consciousness-raising*], reject authority [*by claiming to be God*] and slander celestial beings [*telling us that angels are extraterrestrials from other galaxies or planets*]. But even the archangel Michael, when he was disputing with the devil about the body of Moses, did not dare to bring a slanderous accusation against him, but said, "The Lord rebuke you!" Yet these men speak abusively against whatever they do not understand [*true Christianity and the church*]; and what things they do understand by instinct, like unreasoning animals—[*the spiritual nature of man and life after death, which they take to the extremes of human divinity and reincarnation*] these are the very things that destroy them.

Woe to them! They have taken the way of Cain[*presumptuous forms of worship*]; they have rushed for profit into Balaam's error [*teaching error for profit*]; they have been destroyed in Korah's rebellion [*moral anarchy*].

These men are blemishes at your love feasts [*telling us that Zen meditation can augment the sacraments*], eating with you without the slightest qualm [*claiming that they are still Christians*]—shepherds who feed only themselves [*themselves, themselves, themselves*]. They are clouds without rain [*spiritually empty*], blown along by the wind [*searching and unstable*]; autumn trees, without fruit and uprooted—twice dead [*deceived by their own thinking*]. They are wild waves of the sea, foaming up their shame [*destructive of those who seek God*]; wandering stars [*hopelessly lost in their own understanding*], for whom blackest darkness has been reserved forever. (Jude 8-13)

Jude's view of these "spiritually enlightened" people is both sad and condemning. If they think they are spiritual, Jude tells us that they are laboring under a great misconception. To Jude, the New-Age-breeding Gnostics were not spiritual, but ungodly. Look with what dramatic emphasis Jude makes that point:

Enoch, the seventh from Adam, prophesied about these men: "See, the Lord is coming with thousands upon thousands of his holy ones to judge everyone, and to convict all the *ungodly* of all the *ungodly* acts they have done in the *ungodly* way, and of all the harsh words *ungodly* sinners have spoken against him." These men are grumblers and faultfinders; they follow their own evil desires; they boast about themselves and flatter others for their own advantage. (Jude 14-16, emphasis mine)

Do you get the idea that the Holy Spirit is incensed about Gnostic, New Age philosophers boasting of spiritual enlightenment? Jude's assessment is that their philosophy is nothing more than ungodliness dressed up in the pretentious garb of religious respectability

END TIMES CONSPIRACY?

The closest tie New Age Gnostics can claim to Scripture is in fulfilling the prophecies about Christian heresies which would attempt to weaken Christian faith:

> But, dear friends, remember what the apostles of our Lord Jesus Christ foretold. They said to you, "In the last times there will be scoffers who will follow their own ungodly desires." These are the men who divide you, who follow mere natural instincts and do not have the Spirit. But you, dear friends, build yourselves up in your most holy faith and pray in the Holy Spirit. Keep yourselves in God's love as you wait for the mercy of our Lord Jesus Christ to bring you to eternal life. (Jude 17-21)

Some of my fellow critics of the New Age movement (whose zeal in the battle for truth I greatly appreciate) are convinced that the New Age movement is ushering in the Second Coming of Christ. They firmly believe that the New Age movement is a sign of the End Times; that New Agers are forming a conspiracy to unify the world through one world government based on New Age teaching; and that the goal is ultimate elimination of Christians and Christianity. Although there are some extremists on the fringe of the New Age movement who would subscribe to such a cosmic agenda, this is clearly not the agenda of the average New Ager. Even if such a conspiracy existed, its supposed timetable of takeover at the end of the twentieth century is hardly believable. (One need only look to the militancy of fundamentalist Islam to see that no one-world government is just around the corner.)

It is important to note that Jude was writing to those in his own first-century generation when he referred to the apostles' warnings about scoffers who would come "in the last times." We have been in "the last times" since Jesus appeared on the earth. New Age belief is by no means a metaphysical belief system which, for the first time, has cropped up in our generation. As we have seen, it mimics first-century Gnosticism and has its roots deeply embedded in the sinful soil of the Garden of Eden.

There is no need to turn a spiritually lethal grass-roots philosophical movement into a worldwide political conspiracy. The danger of the New Age movement is unquestionably real, but we aren't going to find a New Age "commie" behind every tree. Jude is not urging an era of spiritual "McCarthyism" at the end of the twentieth century. He is warning *us* not to be deceived by those who scoff at Christ's pure teaching and who would lead us down the path to spiritual destruction. The warning is more for *us* than for *them*. "Build yourselves up in your most holy faith," Jude implores. "Pray in the Holy Spirit." Do not fall for their crystal lies!

As for the time of Christ's coming, Jude isn't concerned about second-guessing God's own timing. "Keep yourselves in God's love as you wait," is Jude's calm advice. Our job is not to predict, but to produce.

Instead of tarring every New Ager with the charge of global conspiracy, Jude points the way toward loving confrontation: "Be merciful to those who doubt; snatch others from the fire and save them; to others show mercy, mixed with fear—hating even the clothing stained by corrupted flesh" (Jude 22, 23).

Not all New Agers are alike. The wide diversity among Christians ought to teach us that. Among New Agers there are hard-core fanatics who believe in the complete array of paranormal phenomena from astral projections to UFO's carrying highly evolved spiritual entities from the astral plane. There are other New Agers who would scoff at such claims, yet believe in the basic premise that they are part of the oneness of the universe—even to being God, if you pressed them.

Still others would deny passionately any notion that they are God. They simply accept that their potential as human beings is enhanced through yoga, meditation, chanting, and other Eastern metaphysical practices. You might even find them seeking the services of a psychic or channeler. On the bottom end of the scale are those who might dabble in astrology, place their faith in holistic healing, or keep a dream journal.

Jude isolates the problem facing many people who are attracted by the New Age movement. For a variety of reasons, they have been caused to doubt traditional Christianity. Whether it was liberal theology which turned them away from Christ, an overbearing authoritative church, or perhaps Christian parents or friends whose lives betrayed true Christian belief—they have come to wonder if Christianity meets their needs. To these, we must be gentle, patient, and understanding.

In the case of those who are caught up in New Age practices, we are to "snatch them from the fire and save them." They are headed for certain trouble if we don't grab their attention and bring them back to their senses. It may take tough words to get the attention of some. If you are wondering how to help someone else resist the temptations of the New Age movement, let me recommend an excellent book, *Confronting the New Age,* by Douglas Groothuis (Inter-Varsity Press, 1988).

DANGER FROM WITHOUT,
DANGER FROM WITHIN

Whatever may be their degree of involvement in New Age thought, Jude warns us not to become involved ourselves as we reach out to others. While we are preaching the error of New Age thought, are we promoting a human potential version of the gospel? Do we in one breath denounce

At The Extremes of Belief / 61

holistic healing and in the next breath advocate the presumptuous "name it and claim it" approach to healing? Do we chide New Age idolatry in the worship of crystals, yet elevate favorite evangelists to high altars of devotion? When we sin willfully, are we not, in effect, joining New Agers in denying the lordship of Christ in our lives?

We must regard our mission of evangelism to New Agers with the greatest of humility, acknowledging our own failings. But we go with courage, knowing that God is with us. Jude's closing remarks put it all into perspective:

> To him who is able to keep you from falling and to present you before his glorious presence without fault and with great joy—to the only God our Savior be glory, majesty, power and authority, through Jesus Christ our Lord, before all ages, now and forevermore! Amen. (Jude 24, 25)

The majesty of Jesus Christ far exceeds anything the New Age movement has to offer. Why should we or anyone want to trade that majesty for a cheap counterfeit like New Age "Christ-consciousness?" Anyone who truly wants to be "in the know" will look, not at his or her own enlightenment, but to him who is the Light of the world—Jesus Christ our Lord.

DIFFERENT KINDS OF GOSSIP

First-century Gnosticism would not prove to be the success that Christianity was to become. It did not have the capacity to fulfill man's quest for transcendence. It could bring a person to a greater utilization of his humanity, perhaps, but no further. More typically, it brought man down to his baser human weaknesses.

One major post-Christian religion is far more successful

and deserves at least passing notice in filling out the scope of the Global Gossip Game in the context of extremist religious belief. Drawing from both Jewish and Christian faith, Islam likewise recognizes the one God but honors Mohammed as God's prophet, not Jesus, the Son of God. One hardly need be reminded of the difference that this choice makes in Islamic cultures. Virtually every front page today reminds us of the Muslim world and its political foment. Where Jesus said, "Love your enemies," Islam says, "Kill your enemies." (The fact that millions have been killed in the name of Christianity does not alter Jesus' teaching against such carnage.) And where Jesus said that the Law was made for man, Islam's legalistic requirements affirm a belief that man was made for the Law.

Comparing Islam with the New Age movement also reveals a sharp contrast. For example, Islam's legalism is certainly an extreme avoided by the New Age movement. In the New Age, there is no law, only moral anarchy. Not even the so-called law of karma seemingly can prevent self-rule. When viewed from the perspective of the New Age movement, Islam's legalism starts to look pretty good. If it often goes overboard in fanatical rule-keeping, at least many of its rules are morally commendable. Unfortunately, the same cannot be said for the standard-less philosophy of the New Age.

A DIFFERENT WORLD VIEW ALTOGETHER

When the game of "Gossip" is played, it sometimes happens that a player will interject a completely different message than the one being passed around the room. When that happens, what the last player hears has no similarity whatever to the original message. This has occurred in the Global Gossip Game as well. When Charles Darwin proposed his general theory of evolution, he interjected a world view that radically altered the Western world's understanding of a creative God. Despite attempts by many believers to reconcile Christianity with Darwin's amoeba-to-man evolution, Darwin himself would have none of it. "Man in his arrogance thinks himself a great work worth the interposition of a deity. More humble and I believe truer to consider him created from animals" (*Charles Darwin,* Peter Brent, Hamlyn, 1981, p. 294).

Darwin's great contribution to science was his discovery of evolution within the various species. His subsequent unproven conjecture that therefore one species must have evolved into other, higher forms left God out of the process. Even the origin of the first living matter, which Darwin at first was willing to attribute to a creative God, in the end became a mystery he did not want to attribute to anything associated with deity. By his own theory, he had become an atheist.

With the widespread acceptance of macroevolution came also widespread disbelief in the Creator God of the Bible. Coming as it did during a time of great social upheaval, the "scientifically-verified" denial of God even contributed to a new political expression. Marxist socialism and its political spinoff communism—both atheist-oriented—became the entrenched beliefs in the Soviet Union and other communist countries formerly dominated by Orthodox Christianity. Even in England, where the church buried Darwin with full honors, an already-weakened church suffered a death blow from which it is still staggering. In the United States, evolutionary atheism has contributed significantly to a dominant social force in the form of secular humanism.

It is significant that the New Age movement is closely tied to Darwinian evolution. The basic idea of the New Age is that we are at the stage in evolutionary progress where man is about to make a quantum leap to a higher level of existence. Evolution of the body promotes the idea of evolution of the soul. In her book, *Out On a Limb,* Shirley MacLaine attempts the connection:

> As I lay in the tub thinking, I wondered how long it would be before scientists would find ways to verify the evolution of the soul in the same way that they verified the evolution of the body.

But this is where New Age belief runs into one of its biggest problems. If evolution is the cause of man's existence, what accounts for the existence of the soul? Evolution concerns itself with the *natural* development of the human body. Man's soul, even by New Age definition, is *supernatural,* paranormal, metaphysical. The soul is a dimension to man altogether different from his body. Before something can *evolve* it has to *be!*

There is yet another difficulty in attempting to reconcile New Age belief with Darwinism. New Agers tell us that we are essentially and fundamentally deity. We are God; we are divine. Once again, Charles Darwin would have none of such thinking. His sympathetic biographer, Peter Brent, says of Darwin, "He turned again to the situation of Man, who 'is not a deity, his end under present form will come (or how dreadfully we are deceived)'" (p. 293).

For Darwin, man was no more than a highly evolved animal, and therefore had no spiritual dimension that would survive death. How can such a fatalistic belief possibly be reconciled with New Age belief in reincarnation of the soul? Despite such incongruity, you still hear New Age proponents attempting to draw on Darwin for support of their belief system.

In the closing chapter of his Darwin biography, Brent suggests "It is hard not to believe that Darwin's first vision was one that realized even as it defined the unity of all things." You mean that Darwin, like New Agers, believed that all is one? Yes, says Brent: "Those who have travelled to the limits of human spirituality bear witness that their reward is a direct awareness of an underlying cosmic unity" (pp. 514, 515). One can only wonder what Darwin would think of this New Age spiritual gloss given to his emphatically naturalistic conclusions about man and his universe.

Given a choice, I would honor Darwin's consistency of belief over the New Age's futile efforts to reconcile the irreconcilable. But the only *true* way to reconcile God, the universe, and man is to honor the scriptural revelation of the mind of God who made man and his universe. By their frenzied commuting back and forth from the extremes of metaphysical Gnosticism and Darwinian evolution, New Agers have shown themselves to be anything but enlightened. They are hopelessly confused, like a child accused of doing something wrong blurting out a host of contradictions in an attempt to get off the hook. Their smorgasbord of faith cannot be fulfilling. It is serving up the most serious of all deceptions—self-deception.

SIX

The Reincarnation Myth

A S I LOOK OUT onto the peaceful front garden of the little English cottage where I annually retreat from the hectic pace of America, it is spring again. And the puffy white clouds racing over the green hillside look just like yesterday's clouds making a return visit. Following a mild winter, already there are tiny primroses, snowdrops, and purple crocuses blooming in the rockery. And last spring's daffodils are promising a return performance of splashing yellow. Soon, they will be the very picture of an English garden in springtime.

The verdant hillside rising beyond the garden hedge is empty now. The sheep are gone. But soon it will be lambing time, and the little lambs and their mothers will be brought to pasture once again. The whole earth is breathless with anticipation. One can hardly look out on nature's landscape without being impressed with the never-ending cycle of life. Each day is an eternity in microcosm. Each season a reminder of seasons past. Each year a time for renewal.

Yesterday, I watched with interest as a kindly old woman walked slowly up the village lane, pushing a tram with a pretty little girl, whose honey blond tresses blew gently in the cool breeze. They stopped occasionally to look at a flower or a bird or just a puddle of water. There were questions from the younger generation, and grandmotherly wisdom from the older generation. And in that moment, life was as it should be. The mysteries of life were being passed from one generation to the next. It's been that way since we can remember. And even before that, of course. As the older folks leave us, the young are born to take their place. Death and life go on in an endless rhythm.

One could be forgiven, then, for believing that we, too, come and go. That we make return performances. That we live many lifetimes on this earth.

WISHFUL THINKING

There are times when we look into the mirror and see telltale signs that make us want to run screaming back into our youth. Perhaps it's the wrinkles or the gray hair. Perhaps it's having no hair at all! "If only I could be young again," we sigh. Or there's that time of challenge to which we had looked forward with such anticipation, only to fail embarrassingly. "Oh, if only I could do it over again!" we lament. "Could I have a second try?"

Pity all of us who have ever lost a loved one. "If only he could come back again," we mourn. "If only she could walk back through that door just one more time." Or maybe it is the man who has just retired after fifty years of doing a job he hated, or a woman who has lived with an abusive husband, year after agonizing year. "If only my life had been different . . ."

One could be excused, then, for wishing that we could come back into the world and start fresh, apply ourselves more seriously the next time around, have a different hand dealt to us.

LOOKING FOR EXPLANATIONS

When a child is born with a physical or mental handicap, the immediate question is, "Why?" When the shiny new car is off in the ditch and every fender is bent, one wonders, "What did I do to deserve *that?*" Let a man unexpectedly leave his wife for another woman, and a never-ending parade of self-interrogation passes through her mind: "Could I have done something to keep him from leaving?" "What did I do wrong?" "What is there about me that he didn't like?" "What does she have that I don't have?"

Give the single person a particularly lonely day and it won't be long before the questions surface: "Why have I never married?" "What's wrong with me?" Look into the darkened house down the street where that sweet couple lived with such happiness until he died, and if you are really quiet, you can hear a saddened widow ask, "But why must I be left alone?" "Why did he go first?" "Why couldn't it have been me?" "Why couldn't we have gone together?"

When we look around us and see that drinking too much causes accidents on the highway and that eating too much causes us to be overweight, we are comfortable in believing there is cause and effect. Hurricane winds blow in from the gulf and houses fall down. We are not surprised. The skies withhold rain for months on end and the crops fail. It's what we could have predicted. Cause and effect is all around us—even in those syrupy *Sound of Music* lyrics, "Somewhere in my youth or childhood I must have done something good" (Why else am I so happy?).

It would be understandable, then, for a person to wonder if his circumstances or her relationships in life had been determined by something they either had done or failed to do. To wonder whether some law of cause and effect were as active in the moral world as the law of cause and effect in the physical world, where for every action there is an equal reaction. To believe in a law of karma which presumes to answer questions about human suffering and about why babies are born impaired. To want the peace of mind that comes with *some* explanation, *any* reason, even if it is wrong.

LOOKING FOR BETTER ALTERNATIVES

To many, the idea of hell is unthinkable. What kind of a God could punish a person with eternal burning and suffering? How evil would one have to be to deserve such treatment? Can we really believe (as some people suppose) that a person in darkest Africa who has never heard about Jesus Christ can be sentenced to an eternity of condemnation?

And who really wants to go to heaven? Doesn't it sound terribly boring up there? Could it possibly be better than living in Beverly Hills with bags of money? Could it be better than even a walk on the beach at sunset with someone you love? And what about those angelic wings? Aren't they going to be a bit inhibiting? If all that were not enough to put a person off, think about the harp playing and singing. Just nonstop harp playing and endless years of singing! Even the most boring life on earth seems to have an edge on "endless years the same."

When some people think of a great day of worldwide judgment, it seems to them almost unchristian. Didn't even Jesus tell us it's wrong to judge? Besides, I'm the product of my parents and their parents. If I have free will, I'm also wearing some pretty ancient and frazzled genes in my makeup. My actions are affected by the gravitational pull of the moon, PMS, unbalanced nutrition, the "greenhouse effect," and the stress of freeway commuting. How could anyone possibly hold me accountable?

One could gather some sympathy, then, for wanting to

avoid judgment. For thinking that many lifetimes on earth—no matter how bad one's circumstances—sounds better than punishment in hell. For wondering if heaven on earth in the affluent twentieth century doesn't beat the popularized picture of heaven that typically is painted for us. For looking within one's self and realizing that one isn't ready to face a final exam on Life. Or even for wanting to avoid judgment because we are not certain how God will view all the competing forces which have combined to shape our lives.

IT SEEMS SO PROGRESSIVE

Having grown up in a world that accepts the evolution of all things, evolution of the soul makes sense. Even when you look back through biblical history you see what appears to be moral evolution. Eye-for-eye under the laws of Moses gives way to doing good to our enemies under the law of Christ. The God-ordered killing of men, women, and children in the Old Testament is put aside in favor of the New Testament's injunction that we love those who hate us. Where God treated the people of Israel as morally infantile—using a parental style of "thou shalts" and "thou shalt nots"—Jesus approaches his own generation as mature enough to understand the motive-directed fulfillment of the law: "you have heard it said . . . but I say unto you."

Even when we look around at the nonspiritual world, we see quantum leaps in education, science, and technology. We've been to the moon now, and it was "One small step for man; one giant step for mankind." In the age of computers, what we can accomplish is only now being tapped. When medical science can bring people "back to life" after minutes of being "clinically dead," what limits are there to man's immortality? It's not just a matter of having highly advanced equipment and scientific insight. What's important is that we are advancing in our understanding and our command of the universe at rates of geometric progression. What began with hesitant crawls and falls has become progress by leaps and bounds.

It could be seen as being in step with the times, then, to believe that we are on the threshold of a whole new way of thinking about life and afterlife; that human intelligence has brought us to the brink of superlearning and super-knowledge, outstripping the myths of ancient Scriptures which teach that we live only once; that "afterlife experiences" prove life after death and make reasonable the possibility of reincarnation.

WHAT PROOF OF REINCARNATION?

For these and other reasons, the idea of reincarnation—that we live many times on the earth in different bodies and personalities—has been a central belief of many world religions. But where is the proof that anyone has ever been reincarnated? The Bible tells us that people have been brought back miraculously from death by Old Testament prophets, by Jesus and his apostles, and upon the occasion of Jesus' own crucifixion. All this by the power of God. But in each instance, apart from Jesus himself who ascended into heaven, the person came back into his or her former body, died once again, and never reappeared in that or any other body. A far cry from multiple reincarnations!

Where were you when you first learned that the space shuttle "Challenger" had exploded? Were you watching the television screen as it went up in flames? If you are old enough, do you remember what you were doing the day President Kennedy was assassinated? Some of you who are older also have etched into your memory "a date that will live in infamy," the bombing of Pearl Harbor by the Japanese, or perhaps the Allied invasion of Normandy on D-Day.

But do you remember where you were when President Lincoln was assassinated? Or when William the Conqueror invaded England in 1066? Or when Jerusalem was sacked by the Roman legions? Are the details of those events etched into your memory? Of course not. But why shouldn't they be if we have all lived many lifetimes throughout the sweep of history?

It's too easy to say that we have difficulty recalling the details of what happened to us last year, or, for some of us, even last week. It's not enough to suggest that most of our childhood memories are locked away in the deep recesses of our minds. We can remember clearly every significant adult experience we have ever had. If we have had lifetimes of adult experiences, there ought to be some vestige of memory accumulated for recall during this lifetime. But none of us has such recall.

What would be the value of having lived many lifetimes if we can't remember who we were or what we did? How are we ever going to evolve spiritually if we can't learn from the mistakes of the past? What's the use of karma if we don't know what bad karma we are trying to overcome? Knowing our past lives may be fun and games, but what has it done for us lately?

Some New Agers tell us that we see the accumulation of many lifetimes of knowledge in child prodigies, those rare geniuses of music and the arts at early ages. But even the child prodigy has to learn to tie his shoelaces! And why would child prodigies be the exception rather than the rule? Have we not all had hundreds, if not thousands, of past lives according to New Age belief? Without memory of past lives and the benefit of accumulated knowledge, the idea of soul progression becomes meaningless.

Where is the evidence for soul progression through reincarnation in human nature? Ever since Cain killed Abel, we have had one murder after another. From the first rock thrown in anger to the development of the H-Bomb, man has made war against his fellow man. And how, after so many centuries of reincarnation and soul progression, could we possibly have developed an Adolf Hitler? Closer to home, why in our own backyards do we find dishonesty, crime, drug and alcohol addiction, child abuse, and racial and economic oppression?

Moreover, what possible benefit has reincarnation been in the lives of the millions of people in India? They continue to live in abysmal suffering and deprivation despite the dominance of two world religions which honor reincarnation as man's progressive evolution to enlightenment. India is a case study in the embarrassing failure of any supposed reincarnation. Stagnation, repression, poverty, and discrimination are the legacies of reincarnation belief—not progress, cosmic enlightenment, or raised consciousness; not even social responsibility.

AN EVEN WORSE ALTERNATIVE

Reincarnation is the third of the major afterlife explanations. The first option is given to us by the secular humanists: there is no life after death. When we die, we no longer exist in any form or dimension whatever. "Like little dog Rover, we are dead all over." This conclusion naturally follows from acceptance of the Darwinian world view in which there is no God and wherein man has no soul.

This has also been the predominant afterlife view held by secular Jews of today. Afterlife theology has never been Judaism's strong suit, and so it is not surprising that a rather cynical fatalism has been embraced by most twentieth-century Jews. Nor is it surprising that among both secular humanists and the Western world's secular Jews, thousands have accepted the New Age movement's belief in reincarnation. It gives them hope for life after death. And as a bonus, they don't have to worry about the possibility of judgment and hell.

The second option, which secular humanists' reject, is the Christian view of resurrection. Naturally, there are good reasons for rejecting resurrection. As mentioned, it leads to a moral judgment of our life on earth, gives no second chances, and submits us to the risk of punishment. It also forces us to take seriously the claim of Jesus that he was God in the flesh with the power to overcome death. If he really was who he said he was, then we are forced to come to grips with his call for moral purity, self-sacrificing righteousness, and denial of the material world's enticement. It's a high price to pay for anyone who is unwilling to give up self-determinism. But the fact of Jesus' resurrection, foreshadowing our own resurrection, is difficult to deny.

WHAT EVIDENCE FOR RESURRECTION?

Within hours, a recent precautionary trip to my doctor to check out slight chest pains quickly generated rumors of a heart attack, resulting in calls as far away from California as the East coast. Fortunately, as with Mark Twain, the rumors of my death were greatly exaggerated.

Is it likely that rumors of Jesus' resurrection were also greatly exaggerated? Given the nature of rumors, it is altogether possible that the slightest mischaracterization of Jesus' death and burial might have generated visions of a risen Lord. But as a former trial lawyer, I wonder whether we could take seriously the idea that Jesus' resurrection was the result of mere rumor.

No one who passed along the rumor of my "heart attack" would have vouched for his information at risk to his own life, but that is exactly what the witnesses to Jesus' resurrection were willing to do. And some of them literally had to die in defense of their testimony. That's what I call credibility!

As with many who called my home to verify the news

they had heard, those who had only second-hand information about Jesus' resurrection demanded hard evidence of such an extraordinary claim. You'll recall how Thomas doubted the rumor until Jesus invited him to touch the wounds of his resurrected body in that upper room in Jerusalem. That was certainly believable evidence for Thomas and ought to be for us as well.

"But," someone might say, "that is only a story told by Jesus' disciples to bolster a belief which they conjured up in order to keep Jesus' ministry alive in the public mind. It is only hearsay." But even hearsay may be admitted in court when it passes the test of being trustworthy and reliable. And in the four Gospels we have written accounts penned so close in time to the alleged resurrection appearances that any fraud would easily have been exposed by Jesus' enemies. For example, you can rest assured that the unbelieving Jews would have rushed to produce Jesus' body had the disciples simply been making up the story.

Corroboration is one of the most persuasive forms of evidence that an advocate can produce. In the case of Jesus' resurrection, we find Jesus appearing after his death and burial, not to just one person, but to many persons over many days and in many different locations. On at least one occasion, Jesus appeared to over 500 people at one time! Surely that would eliminate any possibility that any one person might have been seeing an apparition or hallucinating some spiritual appearance. Surely also, it would prevent zealous disciples from tricking some lone gullible person into believing that Jesus had escaped the bonds of death.

"But could all of this testimony not simply be a legend promoted by Christ's followers?" asks another. Legend experts tell us that it takes at least two generations for legends to be established. It is significant, then, that the story of Christ's resurrection was being told to those who wrote three of the Gospels within only a few short years after the alleged event. It was also recorded by John, an eye-witness to the resurrected Jesus, within John's own lifetime. If circumstantial evidence sometimes leaves us less certain than we would like to be, what about the testimony of an eyewitness! Surely that is the most reliable evidence we could ever have.

Simplicity is also one of the features of the Gospel testimonies which lends credibility to the historical fact of Jesus' resurrection. Legends, myths, and outright lies tend to be embellished for greater support. But the testimony regarding Jesus' death, burial, and resurrection is straight-forward, simple, and consistent with a person's common perceptive capabilities. In short, the truth of Jesus' resurrection is better than any fiction which someone might have attempted.

If you were trying to impress a jury with what seems to be an incredible story, you would want to present the most credible witnesses you could produce. In Jesus' day, the testimony of women was not legally admissible. Therefore it is all the more unlikely that anyone attempting to perpetrate a fraud on the public would have put women on the witness stand as being the first to encounter Jesus after his resurrection. Not even Jesus' disciples were willing initially to believe the women. But soon there were just too many appearances to too many people in too many places to ignore their testimony. Jesus had indeed risen from the dead!

Sometimes a questionable claim is so ludicrous that credibility is gained from the very fact of its outrageousness. In the case of Jesus' resurrection, who ever would have thought it up? Despite Jesus' many allusions to his coming resurrection, the Jewish mindframe of his own disciples could not grasp the possibility of such an occurrence until Jesus actually appeared to them. Before his appearance, their only conception of "resurrection" was a mostly-vague raising of the physical body at the end of the world. It would never have occurred to them that Jesus could have been raised before that time. And if his own disciples were not the source of such a revolutionary idea, who would have been?

Is the bodily resurrection of Jesus an outrageous idea? Absolutely. But is it also believable? The truth is that it would take more faith to believe that it did *not* happen! An honest look at the evidence will support the Gospels' claim that Jesus died, was buried, and rose triumphant over death—never to die again.

As for Jesus, the rumors of his death *without* resurrection are more than just greatly exaggerated. Those rumors are a denial of the one fact in all of history that guarantees you and me the same hope of conquering the inevitable enemy of death. When even the mildest of chest pains reminded me of the frailty of life, it was the ultimately believable fact of Jesus' resurrection that gave me peace.

THE TRUTH ABOUT AFTERLIFE

Reincarnation is wishful thinking. It is a myth. It is what someone dreamed up to give easy answers to difficult questions, like human suffering. It is someone's way to avoid being judged for his actions while in this world. It is an unproven theory about how our world gets increasingly better through soul progression. It is a denial of the greatest event in the history of the world—the resurrection of Jesus. It is a denial of our own resurrection to life after death without having to face again the pain and suffering of this life.

We often hear New Agers quote the Bible in support of their beliefs, but the one verse you will never hear quoted comes from the writer of Hebrews, who tells us plainly, "Man is destined to die once, and after that to face judgment" (Hebrews 9:27). Reincarnation is one of the greatest of all the crystal lies. It robs us of the importance of our one lifetime on this planet and deceives us about our chances for "getting it right" the second time around. The beer commercial is right: "We only go around once."

SEVEN

Tuning in the Wrong Channels

O UR INABILITY TO REMEMBER past lives has spawned an entire industry of psychics and channelers, ready and waiting to satisfy our every curiosity—for a fee, of course. These clever charlatans are the snake oil salesmen of the New Age. In the spirit of the Bush administration, I wish there were kinder and gentler words to describe them. Certainly, Christianity has had its own brand of hucksterism over the years, and, unfortunately, Christian television continues to promote too many people with questionable motives and fund-raising practices. Sadly, the New Age Movement seems intent on not being outdone. Even while mocking the commercialism of televangelists, New Agers are shelling out more money per psychic channeling session than most Christians donate in a year in support of Christian television. The New Age has become big business.

In search of truth, I went undercover to see for myself. As part of my research for the writing of *Out On a Broken Limb*, I arranged to participate in two sessions given by Shirley MacLaine's psychic, Kevin Ryerson, of San Francisco. You may remember that he played himself in her television adaptation of *Out On a Limb*. Ryerson touts himself as an up-to-date Edgar Cayce. However, Cayce simply went "within himself" to get in touch with his claimed psychic powers. Ryerson claims to be a conduit for astral-plane entities who provide him with his psychic information.

Some months following my investigation, when I appeared with Ryerson on CNN's *Crossfire*, Ryerson told the viewing audience that he had been aware of my mission during his channeling sessions and that I had been openly disruptive among the group. Of course, that was yet another crystal lie. Obviously, the whole point of going undercover is to participate undetected in order to observe the proceedings without coloring them by one's known purpose. But truth is hardly a channeler's stock in trade. What is true is that Ryerson was attempting whatever damage control he could muster. My reporting of his scam had disclosed gross public deception.

My first meeting with Ryerson came when I joined twenty other people in a private home in Southern California for one of Ryerson's New Age lecture and channeling sessions. The crowd of trendily dressed, upper-middle-class Californians arrived in BMW's and Mercedes Benzes. The atmosphere was warm and inviting, much like Christians would experience in a house church setting. During breaks, we mixed informally in the kitchen, munching on rice cakes, peanut butter, and honey.

As the session got under way, Ryerson casually and competently unwrapped the basic New Age package of beliefs for the uninitiated. He obviously was knowledgeable in the fields of psychology, world religions, philosophy, metaphysics, and history of the occult. In that, he rose far above the typical $10 palmist or aura expert at the local psychic fair. It was not difficult to see how easily he could gain a person's confidence. Add to that a healthy, boyish look and a laid-back style coupled with humor, and you had a master of deception poised for the kill.

DEMONS OR A VIVID IMAGINATION?

Lecture ended, Ryerson prepared to go into what he claimed to be a trance state in order to become a human telephone to two supposed entities on the astral plane. These entities—highly-evolved, disembodied spirits—were said to be volunteer spirit guides helping us along on our spiritual journeys. Being in touch with the omniscient Akashic Records—that great cosmic computer "out there" which sees all and knows all—they were prepared to tell us virtually anything we might want to know. Whether it be past lives, the inside scoop on personal relationships, health or dietary concerns, stock market trends, or further insight into New Age philosophy, the entities could do it all. For the price of admission, we had omniscience at our fingertips.

The first entity, "Tom," was billed as an Irish pickpocket in one of his prior lifetimes. Why, as a current resident of the astral plane, he continued to speak in an Irish brogue (a particularly *bad* one at that) was never clarified. "John" was far more cultured, sporting an Elizabethan accent reminiscent of the King James Version of the Bible. Accordingly, John's messages were sprinkled liberally with "thee" and "thou," and the obligatory "cometh" and "goeth." "Tom" and "John" seemed to break into each other's presentations from time to time, maintaining the same New Age content while varying the style.

One of the primary reasons for my attendance at Ryerson's session was to determine as best I could whether his work was actually demonic. Having never before experienced demonic activity, I wasn't exactly sure what I was looking for. But I ventured that I would recognize it if I saw it. It took no more than Ryerson's so-called entry into the trance state to convince me that demons could take a night off. Ryerson's movements were slick, but far too theatrical to convince me that he was in what fairly could be called a trance state.

When I think of demons, I think of the word *shudder.* "Tom" and "John" didn't make me shudder. If anything, their obvious histrionics made me want to laugh. And to cry. Twenty bright, well-educated people were taking it all in, as if everything were real. Their conversations with "Spirit," as the entities were to be addressed, were as real for them as if they were talking to you or me.

I have no doubt that Satan, the Great Deceiver and the Father of Lies—crystal or otherwise—is behind all of the channeling that is being used to deceive the unwary into abandoning their faith in God. And I don't doubt that demons can and do participate in such deception. Demons are not make-believe entities like Ryerson's "Tom" and "John." Demons are deadly real. But with talented deceivers like Ryerson on their team, Satan and his demons can take a vacation. Channelers are doing the devil's work for him. And America's sophisticated but gullible generation of lost souls is easily being led down the broad path that leads to destruction.

TESTING THE SPIRITS

Not all spirits are good spirits. In his first epistle, John tells us that we must not accept everyone who claims to bring us spiritual truth.

Dear friends, do not believe every spirit, but test the spirits to see whether they are from God, because many false prophets have gone out into the world. This is how you can recognize the Spirit of God: Every spirit that acknowledges that Jesus Christ has come in the flesh is from God, but every spirit that does not acknowledge Jesus is not from God. This is the spirit of the antichrist, which you have heard is coming and even now is already in the world. (1 John 4:1-3)

Ryerson and his supposed spiritual entities flunked the test. While they recognize the historical person of Jesus and regard him as a highly-evolved spiritual entity—perhaps the most highly evolved ever—they do not acknowledge that he is the one and only Son of God. In fact, they blasphemously claim the possibility of achieving his status as Christ, and that we ourselves are God. In a sense, Ryerson's entities *are* from God, at least as he defines *God*. His entities clearly come from within himself, from his own vivid imagination.

"Testing the spirits" in that deceptively comfortable living room that night was not a difficult task. Before going "into trance," Ryerson invited us to ask "Spirit" about any dreams we may have had. "Spirit" supposedly could interpret our dreams for us. As we took turns around the room, one woman had a particularly difficult time relating her dream. The parties involved in the dream became so confusing that "Tom" was getting upset trying to sort them all out. His confusion intrigued me. When it came my turn, I asked, as if naive, "Spirit, why is it that you can tell us the interpretation for our dreams, but cannot tell us the dream itself?" "Spirit" answered that, certainly, that could be done, but "it would tire the instrument [meaning Ryerson] to do so." I thought to myself, "We're paying good money for the experience. Let's wear him out!"

The truth is that neither Ryerson nor any other New Age channeler—even with the help of their supposed spiritual entities—has the ability to tell us what we have dreamed. Their inability to know our dreams is an Achilles' heel that only serves to dramatize the fraud of their inventive interpretations.

THE ACID TEST FOR CHANNELERS

My test of the spirits in this instance, of course, was taken directly from the biblical experience of Daniel, to whom God had given the power to interpret dreams. During the Jews' exile under Babylonian captivity, around 600 B.C., King Nebuchadnezzar wanted one of his dreams interpreted by the psychics in his royal court. But Nebuchadnezzar was no fool. As a test of the accuracy of interpretation, he insisted that he first be told the dream itself. If someone could tell him his dream, then surely he would have the power to give the king the correct significance of the dream. Not unexpectedly, none of his in-house psychics could tell him the dream.

The importance of this acid test for modern-day channelers, psychics, and clairvoyants warrants a retelling of the story:

In the second year of his reign, Nebuchadnezzar had dreams; his mind was troubled and he could not sleep. So the king summoned the magicians, enchanters, sorcerers and astrologers to tell him what he had dreamed. When they came in and stood before the king, he said to them, "I have had a dream that troubles me and I want to know what it means."

Then the astrologers answered the king in Aramaic, "O king, live forever! Tell your servants the dream, and we will interpret it."

The king replied to the astrologers, "This is what I have firmly decided: If you do not tell me what my dream was and interpret it, I will have you cut into pieces and your houses turned into piles of rubble. But if you tell me the dream and explain it, you will receive from me gifts and rewards and great honor. So tell me the dream and interpret it for me."

Once more they replied, "Let the king tell his servants the dream, and we will interpret it."

Then the king answered, "I am certain that you are trying to gain time, because you realize that this is what I have firmly decided: If you do not tell me the dream, there is just one penalty for you. You have conspired to tell me misleading and wicked things, hoping the situation will change. So then, tell me the dream, and I will know that you can interpret it for me." (Daniel 2:1-9)

Is there a conspiracy associated with the New Age movement? When it comes to deceiving us through a growing army of psychics, astrologers, and channelers, the answer is a resounding *yes!* By giving us vague, fortune-cookie predictions and dream interpretations that easily could happen to anyone, they are misleading us into thinking that they have the true answers to life's most serious questions.

To their credit, Nebuchadnezzar's resident psychics finally admitted that they could not deliver what they advertised:

> The astrologers answered the king, "There is not a man on earth who can do what the king asks! No king, however great and mighty, has ever asked such a thing of any magician or enchanter or astrologer. What the king asks is too difficult. No one can reveal it to the king except the gods, and they do not live among men." (Daniel 2: 10, 11)

The lesson here is never to trust anyone who claims to be able to interpret your dreams but can't tell you the dream in the first place. Only God would have the power to do that. In the case of Nebuchadnezzar, God demonstrated his power through his servant Daniel, a Jewish captive in Babylon. Daniel did not go into a trance, as New Age channelers do. After praying to God for God's revelation of the dream and its interpretation, Daniel was brought before the king.

> The king asked Daniel (also called Belteshazzar), "Are you able to tell me what I saw in my dream and interpret

it?'' Daniel replied, "No wise man, enchanter, magician or diviner can explain to the king the mystery he has asked about, but there is a God in heaven who reveals mysteries. He has shown King Nebuchadnezzar what will happen in days to come. Your dream and the visions that passed through your mind as you lay on your bed are these . . . (Daniel 2:26-28)

Daniel then related Nebuchadnezzar's dream and proceeded to give him the correct interpretation. (The accuracy of the interpretation is seen in the subsequent history of the rise and fall of four world powers—hardly the kind of interpretation that could be contrived.) Nebuchadnezzar's response points us back to the only source of spiritual insight we can trust—the God of Creation:

> "The great God has shown the king what will take place in the future. The dream is true and the interpretation is trustworthy."
> Then King Nebuchadnezzar fell prostrate before Daniel and paid him honor and ordered that an offering and incense be presented to him. The king said to Daniel, "Surely your God is the God of gods and the Lord of kings and a revealer of mysteries, for you were able to reveal this mystery." (Daniel 2:45-47)

The power of God is revealed in his ability to know all things, even the secrets of our minds. The weakness of New Age psychics is revealed in their inability to tell us the secrets locked within us. And the implications are even greater. If a New Age medium or channeler is willing to deceive us about our dreams, it is likely that he is also willing to deceive us about the truth of his New Age message.

At the close of a trial, the judge may instruct the jury that "A witness found to be intentionally false in one part of his testimony is to be distrusted in all other parts of his testimony." New Age channeling is not an innocent pastime. Psychic "Tupperware" parties run by popular, entertaining personalities are a monument to the deception of the New Age. Small crystal lies betray larger crystal lies.

TRAPPED BY THEIR OWN DECEPTION

Having put "Spirit" to the test proposed wisely by Nebuchadnezzar, I asked "Spirit" to interpret an actual dream I had had about Shirley MacLaine and myself. Months of being totally immersed in her writings and her New Age philosophy had led my mind to concoct a vividly remembered scene involving the two of us in Malibu, where we both live. The scene was in a house along the Pacific Coast Highway by the ocean. "Spirit's" interpretation was predictably vague—something about the waves bringing spiritual insight, which Ms. MacLaine and I would share. My radically different world view from Ms. MacLaine's was my first clue that the interpretation was badly off target.

The real clincher, however, came four months later when my name finally reached the top of Ryerson's list for one-on-one channeling sessions. At that session, I guessed that Ryerson would not have remembered me from the prior group session. I also figured that, psychic or no psychic, Ryerson would not know the purpose for which I had come. (Surely, a true psychic *would* know, wouldn't he?) As Ryerson went "into trance," I asked once again for "Spirit's" interpretation of the exact same dream, which I repeated in detail. Already you probably can guess that this time I got a wildly different interpretation! Is truth in the New Age that flexible?

As a further test, I told Ryerson that I really wanted to communicate with my mother. I told him that there were some things I just felt moved to talk to her about. The answer came back, "We do not contact the spirits of the dead, but if you have a dream in which your mother appears, you will actually be talking to her. All of our dreams are real, involving real people. If you want to talk with your mother, look for her in your dreams.''

What Ryerson's "entities" failed to take into account was that my mother is very much alive and well! If I really want to talk to her, I can do so, simply by picking up the telephone. How can we trust those who claim virtual omniscience when they are unaware of the most easily verifiable facts? For those who claim to be able to tell us about our past lives—which, we are told, often interact with the past lives of our parents and friends—knowing whether my mother was dead or alive should have been elementary.

Suppose I had been serious in my inquiry about my mother. I would have been deceived seriously. Suppose a person goes to a New Age channeler, such as Ryerson, with serious questions about the meaning of life and afterlife. He, too, will be deceived seriously. The source is as important as the message. Whom can we really trust?

MONEY TALKS

For my book *Out On a Broken Limb,* I desperately wanted a past life with Shirley MacLaine. She claims to have been incarnated as any number of personalities throughout history, and I thought it would be a nice literary touch to be associated with her somewhere along the way. I was certain that if I merely asked Ryerson for such a past life, I would get it. "'Spirit,'" I ventured forth, "can you tell me why I have such an interest in Shirley MacLaine and her books? Is it possible that, well, maybe we shared our prior lives together sometime?''

Sure enough, I got what I was after. "Spirit's" response was that Ms. MacLaine and I had worked together as associates in the thirteenth century in China. I was a Taoist scholar and she was a shadow puppeteer. Together, we took the message of Taoism to the people.

In the New Age, you can get what you pay for. If you *want* a particular past life, you can have it. If you *think* you might have been Attila the Hun or Joan of Arc, you were. Never mind that others already might have claimed that identity for themselves! Or that you never would have had that particular past life if you hadn't suggested the possibility to your local psychic.

I am reminded here of a particularly apropos passage in Jeremiah's prophesy. The psychic mediums that are typical of the New Age movement were a problem even in his day. But look how he draws us to our own responsibility in the lies that we are told:

> Yes, this is what the LORD Almighty, the God of Israel, says: "Do not let the prophets and diviners among you deceive you. Do not listen to the dreams *you encourage them to have.* They are prophesying lies to you in my name. I have not sent them," declares the LORD. (Jeremiah 29:8, 9)

Jeremiah says that we have no one to blame but ourselves when we believe dreams that we have *encouraged* the psychics and channelers to have. What else should we expect? They are going to oblige us with whatever answers we want. That's what their business is all about—satisfied customers! This also explains why everyone seems to have been some flamboyant or notable historical character in their previous lives. You're not likely to be told that you were some unknown fisherman on the banks of the Zambezi River who died of old age. There's no excitement or honor in that tale!

New Age psychics are no different from the false prophets of Israel who, for a fee, prophesied whatever anyone wanted to hear.

> Her leaders judge for a bribe, her priests teach for a price, and her prophets tell fortunes for money. Yet they

lean upon the LORD and say, "Is not the LORD among us? No disaster will come upon us." (Micah 3:11)

By contrast, Jesus never conducted weekend psychic seminars for $300 per person. He never had channeling sessions to God the Father for $150 a turn. In fact, he never took up a collection at all, that we know of. His supporters gave generously so that his ministry could continue, but his teaching and his miracles were always dispensed for free. (Yes, you're right, Jesus never begged for money or "love offerings," either, or threatened that God was going to call him home if he didn't meet his budget!)

HOW ELSE COULD THEY KNOW?

Often I hear people who are amazed that their personal psychic or channeler has told them things that no mere human could know. For example, Shirley MacLaine was amazed when Ryerson's on-call "Spirit" came up with the name of the lover with whom she was involved in an adulterous affair. "How did he do that?" she wondered. There are at least three distinct possibilities.

Much of the claimed success of nebulous pronouncements by psychics is attributable to accuracy by coincidence. Horoscopes and fortune cookies are sometimes dead right on! When my dinner partner's fortune cookie says she will be with a handsome man, who am I to argue otherwise? And with fortune cookies and horoscopes, no astral-plane spirit guides are even being consulted. The human experience is just common enough that someone, somewhere will fit the picture presented.

The second possibility is far more formidable. If demons sometimes take a day off, on other days they are hard at work. If you have been told something that truly no human could ever know, and you are sure that it is more than mere coincidence, you may be hearing from sources that ought to send chills down your spine. Satan is active in this world. And he is a liar. So if to deceive you it takes Satan's using a New Age psychic or channeler to tell you something he otherwise could not know, then that information just might come through his lips. Even if he thinks he is just putting you on, he too may be deceived. Once channelers open themselves up for business as human telephones, they might just hear from an unexpected area code!

A third possibility ought to be obvious to Shirley MacLaine and others who may have consulted a channeler, as I did with Kevin Ryerson. Before going into his "trance," Ryerson spent some time with me going over the questions I would be asking "Spirit." He wanted to help me structure my questions for best results, Ryerson said. I suppose that if you really believe Ryerson goes into a trance and has no control over what "Spirit" is saying to you, then you might believe the sincerity of his assistance. You might also believe that the awaiting entity was not a party to your earlier conversation with the channeler.

On the other hand, if the channeler is not going to be hearing from any disembodied spirit guides as he pretends, then the pre-trance warm-up is his chance to get his act together. Why would it matter that you organize your questions properly, except to give the psychic time to come up with the answers you want to hear? The channeled entity and the channeler are one and the same. Why, then, should anyone be surprised that "Spirit" happened to know something that has already been told to the medium?

Once again, the prophet Jeremiah is instructive:

"I have heard what the prophets say who prophesy lies in my name. They say, 'I had a dream! I had a dream!' How long will this continue in the hearts of these lying prophets, who prophesy the delusions of their own minds? They think the dreams they tell one another will make my people forget my name, just as their fathers forgot my name through Baal worship. (Jeremiah 23: 25-27)

If a psychic or channeler tells us something that truly amazes us, it just may be that we are the ones who let the cat out of the bag. Chances are we have just amazed ourselves! Far from knowing our inner secrets, it is their own minds that today's psychics know so intimately. It is from within their own minds that they creatively dream up the crystal lies with which they seduce us.

ENTERTAINMENT, NOT SPIRITUAL CONCERN

One final observation. You will not find New Age mediums warning you about your moral shortcomings or telling you what further discipline you need in your life in order to propel your soul's evolution into a higher realm of enlightenment. For all the talk about karma, whether good karma or bad karma, unfortunately there is little, if any, concern for where you might be headed spiritually.

At the end of my one-on-one session with Ryerson, I asked "Spirit" about my bad karma. "I'm not just interested in my past lives as a matter of curiosity," I said. "I want to find out what my bad karma is so that I can work on it." At that point, Ryerson winced visibly. We had not covered this question in the pre-trance warm-up, and I doubt if he had ever had anyone ask him such a question. It would be a rare person indeed who would go to a psychic because he is seriously concerned about his soul and about what risks he might be facing in future incarnations.

The surprising response from "Spirit" was: "You really don't have any bad karma." Of course I was relieved, but I pressed on, "Then why am I still existing on the earth plane?" "Spirit" answered, "You are to take the message to the people." "Lord willing," I thought, "I hope to do just that." And the message I hope to bring to the people is that New Age belief is a fraud. Sadly, it's often an intentional fraud.

I may not have any bad karma, but I know that I have sin in my life. Too much sin. Sin that needs to be forgiven. And until it is forgiven, sin eats away at us, perhaps unnoticed. No matter how smoothly New Agers or we ourselves might gloss it over, invariably sin brings conflict and hurt. Jeremiah knew that:

> This is what the LORD Almighty says: "Do not listen to what the prophets are prophesying to you; they fill you with false hopes. They speak visions from their own minds, not from the mouth of the LORD. They keep saying to those who despise me, 'The LORD says: You will have peace.' And to all who follow the stubbornness of their hearts they say, 'No harm will come to you.' But which of them has stood in the council of the LORD to see or to hear his word? Who has listened and heard his word? (Jeremiah 23:16-18)

When the New Age movement tells us that we can do anything we set our minds to, in many cases it is giving us false hope. When New Age teachers tell us that we can achieve peace throughout the world and in our own lives simply by visualizing it, they are speaking visions of their own minds, not God's. Peace with God comes through submission to the will of Christ. Peace with our fellow man comes through living pure and righteous lives according to God's divine laws of human conduct. If New Age teachers stood in the counsel of the Lord, they would know that. If they listened to his Word, as many claim to do, they would know that there is no true peace apart from Christ.

Kevin Ryerson was right about there being no bad karma in my life. The same is true of you. In fact, no one has any bad karma. Karma, whether good or bad, is an idea whose time has not yet come. Nor will it ever. If New Age channelers want to give us an inside track to truth and enlightenment, let them talk of sin, separation, and salvation. Let them talk of God's forgiveness. Let them tell us about God's grace. For once, before they destroy us, let them tell us the truth.

EIGHT

Relative Immorality

T HE STUDIO AUDIENCE WAS MESMERIZED; I was horrified. Seated next to me in front of the television cameras, J.Z. Knight was the star of the show, telling us how the 35,000-year-old entity known as Ramtha had mysteriously come into her life; how he had begun using her as a channel through which to bring his cosmic insight to the many thousands of New Age converts who have now attended Ms. Knight's seminars. Charming, witty, and humorous, this extremely attractive New Age heroine was the epitome of femininity—nothing like the strong male personality she assumes when "possessed" by Ramtha. When "clips" of her channeling sessions were shown to the studio and television audience, J.Z. watched the monitor with a reserved smile. I wondered if she saw herself with great curiosity, fascinated with what she looks like when her "soul has left her body," as she claims; or whether perhaps she was amused that so many people took her act seriously. (A former associate quit in disgust after allegedly overhearing Ms. Knight practicing her Ramtha voice in a pre-channeling session warm-up.)

J.Z. Knight's story reads like a Cinderella tale of success. The former cable television executive-turned-guru now commands $200,000 per appearance, charging weekend seminar participants $400 to $1500 per person. She is almost as well known for her Yelm, Washington ranch, complete with a $1.5 million mansion, powder-blue Rolls Royce, and carpeted, crystal-chandeliered stables for her expensive collection of Arabian horses.

Among J.Z's. best-known devotees is Shirley MacLaine, who incorporated Ramtha into her best-selling books. But in a shared taxi ride to the San Francisco airport following the show, Ms. Knight confided that she and Ms. MacLaine had had a falling out. For all the New Age talk of love, peace, and unity, it seems that power politics in the occult kingdom had come between them. But I suppose that is to be expected. It happens with embarrassing frequency in the kingdom of Christ as well.

Having met both Shirley MacLaine and J.Z. Knight, I must say that I was far more impressed with Ms. Knight as a person. Despite my curiosity about her sincerity, there was another sense in which she seemed more genuine, more open. In fact, I commended her for even agreeing to appear on the program, knowing that I had been invited to participate as a critic. It was more than Ms. MacLaine has been willing to do.

REASON TO SHUDDER

Nevertheless, I was far more disturbed by Knight's book *Ramtha* (Sovereign Press, 1986), than Shirley MacLaine's *Out On a Limb*. Where MacLaine's book is fanciful and outrageous, Knight's book is nothing but scary. It is frightening enough to read Marilyn Ferguson's New Age handbook, *The Aquarian Conspiracy*, in which she describes what I believe to be the work of Satan through the New Age movement. But the chilling feeling I had while reading *Ramtha*, was that it *was* the work of Satan!

Ramtha is such a blatant exchange of truth for error that I kept saying to myself, "No human alone wrote this. This book literally could be from the pen of Satan himself." (The book's editor, Steven Lee Weinberg, says that the book is "a collection of edited transcripts drawn from tape recordings of [Ms. Knight's] audiences.") One can only wonder as to the true identity of Ramtha. It could be a figment of Ms. Knight's imagination. It could also be demonic. Quite possibly, it is both.

Whatever its origin, *Ramtha* presents the purest, least disguised doctrine of the New Age movement that I have read. Perhaps this partially accounts for its shocking nature. It also is the least ashamed presentation of the moral chaos fostered by its doctrine, embarrassing as that ought to be. No other book of which I am aware presents so clearly the New Age beliefs that we are God, that we each have our own truth, that we create our own reality, that we choose everything that happens to us, that there is neither good nor evil, that no one has a right to judge our actions, and that we are accountable only to ourselves.

A CASE OF BLASPHEMY

Nor is any book I have ever read so openly blasphemous as *Ramtha*. Just a few excerpts will give you a taste of what I mean:

> Yeshua ben Joseph, whom you call Jesus of Nazareth, is a great god, just as you are a great god. But he is not the only son of God; he is *a* son of God. He was a man who *became* God, just as you will become God. (p. 36)
>
> Yeshua is your brother, not your savior. (p. 37)
>
> A Christ is anyone who realizes that he is God and *lives* that truth. (p. 36)

Love the beautiful entity that you are and the God that
you are—and cease reading your insidious Book [the
Bible]! (p. 38)

In your BOOK OF BOOKS [the Bible, John 1:1] it says:
"In the beginning was the Word, and all was with the
Word." Most improper! The Word was *nothing* without
the Thought, for thought is the basis and creator of
everything that is. (p. 79)

Everything your religions have taught you could be
wrong. Do you know what is wonderful about that? It
means that perhaps there really is no such thing as a devil,
or hell, or sin, or damnation, or a fearsome God—that they
could be wrong. And they *are*. (p. 90)

I hasten to remind you that this teaching comes from one
of the most widely acclaimed spokespersons in the New
Age movement. Nor is it out of line in the least with what is
being taught by others in the movement: God is not God, we
are. Jesus was not the one and only Son of God, and he was
not the exclusive Messiah and Christ of prophecy. We too
can be Christ. And the Bible is deceiving us about every
essential doctrine it proclaims.

Near the end of the program on which J.Z. Knight and I
were guests, the host of the show asked me what was so
wrong with people believing in Ramtha. I got the impression
that he felt it was all very faddish, mere fun and games.
Certainly, it was good entertainment for his own program.
But my heartfelt response was much more serious than he
expected. Referring with a heavy burden to the *Ramtha* book
itself, I told him that we were dealing with nothing short of
blasphemy.

When I mentioned the word *blasphemy*, a distinct hush
came over the audience, and the host did an obvious mental
doubletake. It was only at that point in the program that my
message got a fair hearing. For all their fascination with
channelers, psychics, and the New Age movement, praise

God that among the religiously confused people of America there is still a residual sense of respect for the God of creation and for his revealed Scriptures.

Where that sense of awe and respect is casually tossed out the window, we are headed for certain trouble. You can see it easily in J.Z. Knight's book. There is a predictable progression from the dethronement of God, to the divinity of man, to the abandonment of an eternal judgment, to the exaltation of personal choice, to the denial of good and evil, to the demise of morality.

ON THE DOWNWARD PATH

We have already seen evidence of the New Age movement's central claim that we are God. But it bears repeating because it is the foundation of New Age immorality. Accurately summarizing New Age belief, here is what *Ramtha* tells us about our divinity:

> You are, indeed, divine and immortal entities. (p. 1)
> Whatever man contemplates being, *he will become.* And if he calls himself God, he is going to *become* God. (p. 19)
> Mankind, womankind, humanity—you are God, indeed, wonderfully disguised as limited, wretched entities. (p. 42)
> You want to see what God looks like? Go and look in a reflector—you are looking God straight in the face! (p. 50)
> One day you will... behold God. Touch the Self, that is all you need to do. (p. 50)
> God is not *separate* from you. You and he are *one and the same!* Your will *is* his will. Whatever you want to do *is* what you term "divine providence," divine will. (p. 103)

Already we see the destination: Since we are God, we can do

with impunity anything we want to do. Whatever we do is God's will!

LOSING OUR MINDS

The next step on the downward path is the abandonment of an objective, rational world view in favor of a subjective, intuitive feeling for what is right and wrong:

> I expect you to do only what you *feel* is right. (p. 24)
> There is no voice that will *ever* teach you greater than your own. (p. 27)
> Never believe in anything. Never! That is convincing yourself of something you have yet to know and understand through experience. (p. 57)
> Always trust the wisdom of your feelings. (p. 57)
> And wisdom is not an *intellectual* understanding; it is, indeed, an *emotional* understanding gained from experiencing life. (p. 95)
> Truth is a feeling, a knowingness; it is not intellectual. To know what the truth is for you, is to know what you *feel* the truth is. (p. 111)

Indeed, a person *must* abandon rationality before he can accept that right and wrong are determined by his own feelings. Even if that were to work out satisfactorily for each individual, what would society be like if everyone acted according to their feelings? "It *feels* wrong to go to work today," someone might say. "I think I'll stay home." What kind of national productivity would this encourage? Or, "Overcharging my client *feels* right to me," another might say. Imagine the professional ethics this kind of standard would lead to. Or, heaven forbid, "I'll rape her if I *feel* like it!" Enough said?

The Bible presents a different view, which, perhaps, is why the Bible is so vehemently rejected by New Agers. The writer of Proverbs has at least two thoughts about morality-by-feelings:

He who trusts in himself is a fool,
  but he who walks in wisdom is kept safe. (Proverbs 28:26)

There is a way that seems right to a man,
  but in the end it leads to death. (Proverbs 14:12; 16:25)

It's a little like children insisting on having their own way. "But I *want* to," we hear them say. Like them, what we may want to do or feel like doing, may not always be in our best interest or in the best interest of others. In more than one respect, the New Age would usher us back to a juvenile perspective of infantile self-centeredness and rational immaturity.

MAKE-BELIEVE—THE ADULT VERSION

Like children living in a fantasy world, playing make-believe, so too New Agers tell us that we create our own reality. *Ramtha* says it well on behalf of the movement:

I am here to help you realize that only you, through your sublime intelligence, have created every reality in your life; and with that same power, you have the option to create and experience *any* reality you desire. (pp. 1, 2)

Now, what is God in its most exalted form? Thought. Without Thought, your body would not exist, matter would not exist—*nothing* would exist, for Thought is the creator and supportive element of all life. (p. 31)

You are the one who is wholly responsible for all you have ever done, been, or experienced. You, who have the power to create the magnificence of stars, have created every moment and every circumstance of your life. (p. 45)

Your greatest creations are unhappiness, worry, pity, misery, hatred, dissension, self-denial, age, disease, and death. (p. 47)

This life is all a game; it is an illusion. All of it is! (p. 49)

Life, this grand stage, is your kingdom. It is the platform upon which you create your illusions, your imaginations, your dreams. This wondrous stage affords you the opportunity to dream into existence *any* reality you desire. For the God that you are has the unlimited freedom to dream any thought, embrace the feeling of that thought, and manifest the dream into reality—and anywhere in-between you can change your mind. (p. 95)

You can take from the totality of thought that God is and create any truth, any attitude, any desire you wish. Whatever truth or attitude you create in your thought processes, the Father, Life, readily becomes. (p. 105)

With every successful fraud there is some truth. Indeed, too often we *do* create our own unhappiness by making bad choices. Too often we *do* cause our own problems through worry, stress, unforgiving pent-up anger, living in the past, and violating God's moral laws, which are designed for our own good. But do we create the pains associated with old age? Do we create old age *itself?* Has anyone, through their "unlimited thought processes," been able to remain eternally youthful?

And what about death? Is it really just a thought that would go away if we simply changed our minds about it? Death of the human body is not just an illusion. Nor is the sadness we feel when death comes to someone we love. The death is real, and the sadness is real. When his friend Lazarus died, "Jesus wept" (John 11:35). It didn't matter that Jesus already knew he would bring Lazarus back to life as a demonstration of his unique divine power and of the great truth of life after death. Jesus knew that death is an enemy. The separation it causes cannot help but bring sadness.

There's something else vitally important about the story

of Lazarus. The power of Jesus over Lazarus' death is a power that has not been demonstrated since the first century. Who today can create the reality of life in a lifeless human form? Who among confident New Agers would claim the power to change the ultimate circumstance of death back into life, *days* following burial of the body? The fact of death is no illusion that we can forestall either in our own life or in the lives of others. Physical death is a common enemy. Certain. Unavoidable. Irreversible. Death alone explodes the notion that we are divine entities having the unlimited potential to create our own reality.

Even before death, the fallacy of created reality is seen in our everyday affairs. If we want a new house we don't just stand on a plot of ground and mentally create the reality of a living room in which we instantly find ourselves sitting comfortably. Nor do we "think" into existence a new wardrobe. If New Agers are right about the existence of matter being all in the imagination of the mind (itself "gray matter"), we ought to be able to do those things. And why would we bother to fly on airplanes in order to get from one location to another? Thought control ought to get us from Los Angeles to London without the need for winged planes in the friendly skies. The examples are endless. New Agers are claiming a dimension of creativity and control that they deny each time they take a breath or start their car.

A SUFFERING WORLD WITHOUT VICTIMS

A corollary to the creation of our own reality says that we choose everything that happens to us. There are no accidents, we are told. There are no victims. Again *Ramtha* tells the story best:

> Do you think that things happen to you simply by chance? There is no such thing as an accident or a coincidence in this kingdom—and no one is what is

termed a "victim" of anyone else's will or designs. Everything that happens to you, you have thought and felt into your life. (p. 46)

Only *you* control your destiny. You are the creator of every moment of your life by what you think and feel in this moment. (p. 130)

No victims? How are we going to explain that to the Pan Am passengers who were murderously blown from the sky, or to those who were killed on the ground in Lockerbie, Scotland? Did they *choose* that fatal experience? Do women who are raped *choose* that horrible experience? Do children who are born handicapped *choose* to go through life physically impaired?

Amazingly, New Agers are telling us exactly that! At one of her seminars, Shirley MacLaine was asked, "Do AIDS victims choose to get AIDS?" "Yes," was her answer. Because there is widespread disapproval of homosexuality, it may be necessary for a homosexual to find love and acceptance as a "victim" of AIDS. He chooses that experience in order to surround himself with love before leaving the earth plane.

How about the "victims" of the Holocaust? Did they choose their deaths in Hitler's gas chambers? Again, the answer is *yes. Ramtha* explains it this way:

You may see the slaughter of ten thousand innocents, and you may say, "Woe unto such a misery. Why don't the angels weep for this atrocity? Why do they sing to the glory of God?" Because they have not limited themselves by believing that life ever ends. They know that those who are slaughtered are immediately caught up into "heaven," as you term it, for a greater learning and more experiences and what I call adventures. And though you bury ten thousand bodies and you weep over them, God does not weep. (p. 130)

The Christian can gain comfort in the knowledge that there is life after death, and that heaven can be the hope of those who are innocent victims of atrocities. But they *are* victims. They did not *choose* to be killed, as New Agers tell us so blithely.

How can anyone possibly be drawn to the conclusion that children who are abused *choose* that experience, or give the same explanation for the starving people of Ethiopia or those who died in the Holocaust? How can anyone bring themselves to say that there are no victims? The first answer is that it is so easy to say. In the security and material comfort of a Western world, most of us are *not* the victims of starvation or genocide. But more important, we are forced to say there are no victims in order to maintain the goal that we really want to achieve: *Being in control.* We *want* to choose what happens to us. We *want* to be in charge. If being in charge means that in theory, we choose the bad things that happen to us, then so be it.

If you are like me, you are very happy to be safely on the ground again after a cross-country flight. Given a choice, we would rather be driving home from the airport than sitting up there, bouncing around in the sky. It's no secret that far more people are killed in auto accidents than in air disasters, but despite the greater risk, we are more comfortable when we are in control.

When it comes to how we live our lives, we are likewise more comfortable when we are in control. Given an option, we would prefer to choose for ourselves what is right and what is wrong. We don't stop to think how limited our own vision is. Hardly ever do we remember the disastrous mistakes we have made while insisting on having our own way. The beautiful thing about Christianity is that we realize we are *not* in control. We have a Pilot who guides us safely through life's stormy clouds. We can sit back and relax, and get on with our lives with peace of mind. It's a trade-off, isn't it? Either we can be totally in control and live to regret it, or we can give God control and be certain of our destiny.

I'm as independent as the next person. And I value my God-given freedom of choice. That is why I have chosen not to travel blind. A God who can create me with the ability to choose is the God in whom I want to trust. Trusting in myself is mere arrogance—dangerous arrogance.

NO EVIL, NO WRONG

If we are to choose what happens to us, on what basis will we do so? How will we know what is good for us and what is bad? One of the most surprising links in the New Age chain of beliefs is that there is no right and wrong, no good and evil. Everything just *is*. One might wish New Agers were right about that. It would be nice to get rid of evil so easily. But hold onto your hats. Their doctrine leads to some frightening conclusions:

> Only you have ever determined what is good and what is bad, what is right and what is wrong. (p. 31)
>
> It is only an entity's *attitude* toward something that makes it a beautiful or a vile, evil thing. (p. 105)
>
> In the cosmic make-up of all that is, there is no such thing as evil. (pp. 124, 125)
>
> Since everything is a part of God, if you were to say that any one thing is evil, you would also be saying that God is evil, and he is not. (p. 124)

It is here where New Age thought is betrayed by its belief in monism, that all is one. By making all things one, it has made good and evil to be the same thing and both a part of God. With this equation, New Agers are drawn into the morally bankrupt logical extension of their belief system. At least *Ramtha* is to be commended for intellectual honesty at this point. But take a deep breath and listen in on this recorded conversation (given to us in the book *Ramtha*) between Ramtha and a member of the audience referred to as "Master." Unless you read it for yourself, you probably wouldn't believe it!

Ramtha: Now, Master, do tell me what you think evil is. What is your understanding of bad?

Master: Well, I would say that it's the opposite of good. But mostly what I think evil is, is harming another person.

Ramtha: Indeed? Why is that evil?

Master: Well, for example, if someone harmed my daughter, it's evil because . . . let's say she might die.

Ramtha: That's *your* judgment of evil. But what is evil about dying?

Master: So you don't even think that *killing* someone is evil?

Ramtha: That is correct. . . . your child would not have been destroyed, because nothing can destroy the life of God.

Master: So you're saying that even murder is not wrong or evil.

Ramtha: That is correct . . . Your governments and your religions may try to control the masses with laws and rules and regulations, but they will *never* govern the will of an entity that works in the silence of his own thought processes; only the entity can do that. And if, in the moment, it moves the entity to slay another . . . that entity *needs* to experience that for his purposeful understanding.

And I wish you to understand that the entity who participates with the slayer in his expression is not the victim of the slayer. For perhaps he has contemplated the possibility of being burned, or cleaved in two, or molested. And because he has contemplated it and it is fearsome, he has drawn it right to his doorstep.

Thus the one who needs to slay and the one who needs to be slain—because he needs to understand it—draw each other together . . . for the experience.

Now, there are many who will be horrified, and who will judge and curse the slayer. But I *love* the entity that has slain the other.

The slain will come back, again and again, for life is perpetual, it is continuous.

Murder without evil is monism gone terribly wrong. But it also is monism taken to its logical conclusion: All things are one. Therefore all is God (who is good, not evil). Therefore there is no such thing as evil, and nothing we do can ever be judged to be evil. So Shirley MacLaine is correct when she concludes that since we are God and since everyone's truth is equally valid, "there is no right; there is no wrong." No wrong except, for New Agers, the belief that there *is* right and wrong, good and evil, justice and injustice.

IS NEW AGE IMMORAL?

In *Out On a Broken Limb,* I documented from the movement's literature how cheapened life had become in the New Age. Abortion is justified because the entity in the mother's womb decides at the last minute not to go ahead with a life plan and communicates psychically with the mother in her decision to abort. The sudden infant death syndrome ("crib death") is explained by the newborn entity's change of mind about coming into the earth plane at this time. Suicide is merely deciding to go away for now and to return when cosmic forces are more favorable. Deaths in the Viet Nam war, whether of our soldiers or of the Vietnamese who died from napalm bombs, were all part of a "learning experience" for those entities who died.

It's not just human life that gets cheapened. Kevin Ryerson tells Shirley MacLaine that reincarnation is the cosmic explanation for homosexuality. Since each of us has been both male and female in our various past lives, in a given lifetime there may have been "a rocky transition" from one gender to another. The sex switch got stuck somewhere between "M" and "F" and the entity came out "G" for gay.

And Edgar Cayce's work suggests to his interpreters that acts of adultery may be nothing more than "karmic quickies," deserved by the conduct or attitude of the non-participating spouse. The story-line for *Out On a Limb* was based on Shirley MacLaine's great relief to learn that, in a previous lifetime, the man with whom she was having an adulterous affair had been her husband. So their affair was perfectly acceptable! It hardly matters what society considers to be immoral conduct—whether adultery, homosexuality, abortion, or even murder. In the New Age, where evil does not exist, one can do as he or she chooses without moral incrimination.

In fairness, I've heard no New Ager suggest that we ought to run right out and commit adultery or kill someone we don't like. And most New Agers adamantly deny the charge of moral irresponsibility. They say that personal responsibility is karmically enforced: "We cannot hurt another person without hurting ourselves." But the central doctrines of the New Age movement lead to nothing short of moral anarchy. To use a more technical term, to antinomianism. That is, lawlessness. Once again, *Ramtha* says with boldness what virtually every New Age author and guru concedes:

> This teaching is lawless. It possesses *no laws,* for law is a limitation that obstructs freedom. (p. 25)
>
> God loves you in *complete freedom* to do as you will. (p. 106)
>
> The splendid thing about God is that he is, indeed, lawless. (p. 109)
>
> When others have permitted themselves to be

governed with laws and morals and ideals, you will be a
free entity, for you will belong to no truth but your own.
(p. 114)

Your beloved Father has created no law—save one.
And that law is to express your life according to your own
sovereign will. (p. 122)

Become lawless. That does not equate recklessness. It
simply means taking the rope away from your throat and
allowing yourself to breathe. When you remove yourself
from laws and dogma and limited beliefs, then you allow
yourself to be the freedom and unlimitedness that God is.
(p. 132)

To act nobly is commendable. But by New Age teaching it
is not required. Nor is it naturally promoted. Where Christianity talks about self-sacrifice, self-denial, and self-
control—all of which are attributes of noble conduct—the
New Age movement exalts the Self:

As long as you serve or worship or devote yourselves to
anything outside of yourselves, you will never express the
sublime beauty that you are. (p. 27)

The only way to peace and happiness and fulfillment in
your life is to worship and love yourself—for that is loving
God—and to love yourself greater than anyone else, for
that is what will give you the love and steadfastness to
embrace the whole of humanity. (p. 27)

There is no greater love in life than the love of self. (p.
137)

Jesus did teach that we are to love ourselves, for he taught
us to love our neighbors *as* ourselves (Matthew 19:19). But
self-love comes built-in, even if one's self-esteem sometimes
gets crushed by others. The difficult part is learning to love
others in the same way. Jesus also said, "Greater love has no
one than this, that one lay down his life for his friends" (John

15:13). Self-love is not the greatest love in life. Nor, despite the rhetoric, can self-love lead to embracing the whole of humanity.

SELF-ACCOUNTABILITY: AVOIDING JUDGMENT

Morality without accountability is immorality. In the New Age movement, the only one to whom we are accountable is ourselves:

> For who are you to answer to? No one but yourself. (p. 115)
> Know that you will never have to pay for anything that you have ever thought or done, in this or any life, as long as you forgive yourself for it. (p. 132)

Sometimes when we see someone doing something outrageous, we may say, "Who do you think you are, *God?*" The New Age answer is *"Yes!* I can do as I please, thank you!"

No wonder, then, that New Agers are livid at the thought of God's eternal judgment or such a place as hell. Ramtha assures us forcefully that there is no hell:

> *Ramtha:* What if I told you there is no hell?
> *Woman:* But I've been taught that there *is* a hell, though.
> *Ramtha:* But I'm teaching you there isn't!
> I have looked into the depths of your world, into the center to find a burning lake of fire, and it was not there. And I went to the farthest reaches of your universe to find a place of torment, and it was not there either. And I looked in the same places for a devil and could find him nowhere. And when I returned, I found him in the hearts of those who believe in him and in hell. But there is no such place. (pp. 33, 34)

And he [Jesus] spoke not of hell, entity, he spoke only of life and its beauty. (p. 38)

Of course, the truth is that Jesus did speak of hell—vividly and with warning. In fact, we learn more about hell from the mouth of Jesus than from any other biblical source. The denial of hell is the one crystal lie that New Agers risk meeting head-on with disastrous results!

NEW AGE IMMORALITY

Ideas have consequences. Moral relativism, taught by the American educational system for decades, is now the hallmark of our civilization. Openness, nonjudgmental tolerance, and pluralism have become the only truths of our time. Not surprisingly, therefore, today's generation is ripe for a New Age in which there are no standards, no absolute guidelines, no center stripe down the highway of life, and no accountability apart from one's own choosing, or perhaps the fist that comes back into your own face.

No one should be surprised that Christians often fare no better in the morals department. From widely recognized televangelists who fall in disgrace to all the rest of us, sin smothers us like a blanket. But there is this important difference: Sin is the failure to live up to recognized standards of morality, whereas in the New Age movement there are no moral standards whatever. There are neither moral goals, nor guidelines, nor accountability. Relative truth leads to relative morality. And relative morality leads to immorality

NINE

Questionable Practices in the New Age

A LMOST EVERYWHERE I GO, I am asked about the various practices associated with the New Age movement. Is yoga wrong? Is it alright if I listen to the New Age music playing on my local radio station? What about meditation and chanting? Do dream journals get me into trouble?

It's an exciting new world out there. So many new choices. So many new avenues of self-expression. So many new ways of dealing with modern stress. So much more *need* for inner peace and relaxation. With so many options now available to us, the answer to many of the questions being asked is careful, prayerful discernment. Our choices are not being made in a vacuum. We are caught between two sides in nothing less than spiritual warfare.

If Satan can tempt us with seemingly innocent practices, he thinks he may just get that foothold he is looking for. Perhaps he will settle for simply taking our minds off of Jesus Christ and the power that we can have through him. Perhaps he will accomplish his mission through practices which, for all intents and purposes, even appear to be Christian. More than ever before in our time, we need discernment.

The origin of the Christmas tree is unquestionably pagan. Yet each December I await with eager anticipation the arrival of the fresh cut trees, and of the seasonal aroma my carefully chosen tree spreads throughout the house. Christmas wouldn't be Christmas without a freshly cut tree! None of those plastic imitations for me, thank you. And hardly anything is more fun than trimming the tree, with the blinking multi-colored lights and shiny ornaments. Many of the ornaments have wonderful stories to tell of Christmases past. Call me nostalgic, but each year I pull out the toy train I had as a boy and set it up beneath the tree. When the stockings have been put up on the fireplace mantel and holiday music fills the air, I'm ready to enjoy what for me is the best season of the year.

And yet I am well aware of the pagan origins of Christmas. For me, it's a matter of discernment. Santa Claus, gifts, caroling, the tree, stockings hung with care—all these I enjoy as part of family tradition. But I celebrate Jesus' life each Lord's Day throughout the year, mindful that, during the yule season, Christmas trees and the cross have a tendency to get mixed together, as if they were hewn out of the same forest.

Christmas tradition is not the only heritage we get from pagan practices. The day each week that Christians worship God in a formal way is named in tribute to the sun god. Despite that origin, come Sunday, you'll find us in church singing praise to God and offering prayers in the name of Jesus. We don't stop worshiping on Sunday simply because the name of the day happens to have pagan origins. Again, it's a matter of discernment.

YOGA—EXERCISE OR OCCULT WORSHIP?

How, then, shall we regard the practice of yoga, which is so closely associated with Eastern religions? Is it a worthwhile practice regardless of its pagan origins? Can we participate in yoga exercises without inviting adverse spiritual consequences? Does yoga fall into the same category as Christmas trees and Sundays?

Sharp pains in my left leg recently sent me hobbling to my doctor, who referred me to the physical therapist down the street. Something was said about a sciatic nerve being out of place. It would require stretching exercises and heat treatments. My twice-weekly sessions were a real treat. While the leg muscles were being stretched, Scott, my amiable therapist, and I enjoyed stretching our minds with talk of philosophical and religious questions. He charged for his stretching exercises; I supplied books for my part.

As we neared the end of the treatment sessions, Scott told me I needed to keep up some kind of regular stretching exercises. A smile crossed his face. "Do I dare suggest yoga?" By that time he knew I was cast in the role of opposing virtually all things Eastern, so he figured that would not be my best option. "I'm afraid someone would see you in the lotus position and tell Shirley MacLaine," he laughed.

As it turned out, the pain went away. My stretching takes place now either on a rowing machine or on more pleasant rambles among the sheep up in the hills surrounding the little English village where I spend as much time as possible. The late afternoon walks stretch both my legs and my weary spirit after hours of writing. But yoga might also do the trick. If ever I could get my legs twisted beneath me, I shouldn't have difficulty again with tight muscles. It's a matter of simple physiology. Who cares what you call it?

Or is it really that simple? For New Agers, yoga is serious business. It is not just a value-neutral physical exercise. It's steeped in philosophical, if not religious, significance. Perhaps some background will help demonstrate the connection. Yoga is not simply, or even primarily, stretching. Yoga has more to do with breathing. And breathing has to do with the Hindu idea that universal energy flows from the air we breathe. In fact, the purpose of yoga is to achieve altered consciousness. Its very name *yoga* is derived from the Sanskrit term for "yoke" or "union." Altered consciousness is supposed to lead to a oneness with Brahman, the god force of Hinduism. Thus the ultimate goal of yoga is achieving oneness with deity. The slogan might well be: "Exercise your way to godhood!"

Obviously, if someone happens to be unaware of that connection, then their purpose in doing yoga is radically different. Even so, there are some serious concerns regarding the uninitiated. The first has to do with children and young people, who are becoming involved in yoga exercises at increasingly younger ages. (Teachers like yoga because it helps tone down rambunctious children to within reasonable decibel counts!) With the sweeping acceptance of the New Age movement itself, now is not the time to introduce youngsters to what essentially is a form of Hindu self-worship. When young people become comfortable with the *practice,* they are ripe for conversion to the *philosophy* behind the practice.

Second, even adults are likely to confuse the practice with the belief system upon which it is predicated. The analogy is not exactly parallel, but participating in yoga without being caught up in its ultimate purpose would be something akin to being baptized without relating it to Christ's death, burial, and resurrection. In each case, the practice is supposed to lead to a greater spiritual awareness. Only time will tell in individual cases whether one sees the connection between yoga and New Age belief, and decides that it is a good connection.

Whatever else it may be, yoga is a mystical practice tied to the occult. Unlike Christmas trees and Sundays, yoga is part of an *ongoing* pagan religious practice. Its desired state of complete awareness and tranquility through exercise is being used consciously by millions in order to bring about their own mystical union with Hindu's spiritual god force.

Can a person really participate in yoga without risking complicity with the occult?

The apostle Paul was an advocate of physical exercise. Yet his greater concern was that we exercise the spirit properly. "For physical training is some value, but godliness has value for all things, holding promise for both the present life and the life to come" (1 Timothy 4:8). It is interesting that, immediately preceding this concern, Paul warns: "Have nothing to do with godless myths..." (1 Timothy 4:7). Any physical exercise that deceives us about "both the present life and the life to come" ought to be avoided at all cost.

In his excellent book, *Understanding the New Age* (Word Publishing, 1988), *Los Angeles Times* Religion Editor Russell Chandler asks perceptively, "With so many excellent physical fitness and relaxation practices available, why risk one aligned with Hinduism and altered consciousness?" In the case of yoga, "don't play with fire" seems to be the appropriate caution.

MEDITATION: CHRISTIAN OR PAGAN?

Closely associated with yoga is the New Age practice of meditation. The idea of meditation is to "go within oneself" in search of life's answers. As Shirley MacLaine's spiritual advisors kept telling her, "All the answers are within you." Presumably, one finds enlightenment when he is "focused" on his energy centers, known as *chakras*. Or one may concentrate on his "third eye" in the middle of his forehead. Whatever one's focal point, the object of the meditation is one's own self.

By contrast, when the Bible speaks of meditation there is reflection on God, his love, his laws, and his creation. The psalmist put it into proper perspective:

> Blessed is the man who does not walk in the counsel of the wicked or stand in the way of sinners or sit in the seat

of mockers. But his delight is in the law of the LORD, and on his law he meditates day and night. (Psalm 1:1, 2)

Within your temple, O God, we meditate on your unfailing love. (Psalm 48:9)

I will meditate on all your works and consider all your mighty deeds. (Psalm 77:12)

Oh, how I love your law! I meditate on it all day long. (Psalm 119:97)

I have more insight than all my teachers, for I meditate on your statutes. (Psalm 119:99)

The only other sense in which the Bible uses the word *meditation* is in relation to the reflective attitude of one's heart:

May the words of my mouth and the meditation of my heart be pleasing in your sight, O LORD, my Rock and my Redeemer. (Psalm 19:14)

Nothing in Scripture suggests going inward to find peace or enlightenment from within one's own self. Biblical meditation is focused, not within, but outward on God.

Christian meditation may consist of a person's "quiet time" in the reading of Scripture, in prayer, or in somber contemplation of his life before God. As opposed to the passive nature of Eastern meditation, Christianity stresses active participation in the lives of others. If there are quiet times, they lead, not to one's self, but to others. Or to God, through prayer. In prayer, the Christian communicates directly with God. Sadly, since New Agers believe themselves to be God, in New Age meditation a person ends up talking only to himself.

The *idea* of quiet, reflective meditation is certainly right. How often Jesus himself got away from the pressing crowds and the demands of his ministry in order to seek a time of inner renewal. As one who spends weeks and months substantially alone, delving deeply into the Word and experiencing in a special way the beauty of God's creation, I can testify to the value of meditative periods in my own life. But meditation that is God-directed is far different from meditation that is self-directed.

MANTRAS, CHANTING, AND SINGING

One of the key Eastern religious practices adopted by many New Agers is the chanting of mantras. Mantras originally were Hindu verses chanted metrically. Often now, under both Hinduism and Buddhism, it is a single word or syllable used as an object of concentration. If you've ever heard a group of saffron-clothed Hare Krishnas chanting, you know what this sounds like. Krishna's devotees believe that by chanting the name of God, they can break the hold that karma has over their lives and "go back to godhead," that is, Krishna.

Repetition of God's name gives new and unfortunately perverse meaning to "calling on the name of the Lord." For the apostle Paul, it was a cleansing from his sin that was intended when he was told by Ananias, "Get up, be baptized and wash your sins away, calling on his name" (Acts 22:16). It is obedience that is contemplated by the call to God: "And everyone who calls on the name of the Lord will be saved" (Acts 2:21).

Jesus confronted the issue of chanting head on, contrasting its emptiness with the communication one can have with God through prayer. Immediately preceding his giving of "the Lord's prayer," Jesus warned: "And when you pray, do not keep on babbling like pagans, for they think they will be heard because of their many words" (Matthew 6:7).

Far worse than the "babbling" repetition itself is the

message coming through new Age chanting. In *Dancing in the Light*, Shirley MacLaine explains the use of *Aum*, which, instead of a mantra, she prefers to call an "affirmation":

> Affirmations are spoken resolutions which, when used properly, align the physical, mental, and spiritual energies. The ancient Hindu vedas claimed that the spoken words *I am*, or *Aum* in Hindu, set up a vibrational frequency in the body and mind which align the individual with his or her higher self and thus with the God-source. The word God in any language carries the highest vibrational frequency of any word in the language. Therefore, if one says audibly *I am God*, the sound vibrations literally align the energies of the body to a higher atunement.
>
> You can use *I am God* or *I am that I am* as Christ often did, or you can extend the affirmation to fit your own needs.

First of all, Ms. MacLaine is passing along to us one of the many crystal lies that she has been told by her New Age mentors when she blithely says that the word for God in any language carries the highest vibrational frequency of any word in the language. Perhaps she might convince us with the guttural *gott* (German), but what about *dieu* (French), or *dios* (Spanish), or *theos* (Greek), or *deus* (Latin)? Once again, the attempt to bolster New Age's metaphysical philosophy with scientific verification simply fails the test.

Far more important is the crystal deception of her message. Almost needless to say, it is rank blasphemy: blasphemy in the suggestion that Christ used *"I am God"* as a chanted mantra. And blasphemy in encouraging us to say that *we* are God. The way most of us act each day—as if we *were* God—our morning mantra probably ought to be: "I am *not* God; I am *not* God; I am *not* God!"

For all the yoga, meditation, and chanting, I am intrigued

by a very subtle aspect of the New Age movement. I keep wondering if New Agers don't lack mirth. Look particularly on the faces of those who spend hours each day in a meditative trance and you see a distant, glazed look, with a permanent, almost pasted-on mystical half-smile. I realize this is a subjective, personal judgment—perhaps biased—but the joy I see in the lives of active, committed Christians seems to be missing in most New Agers I have known. New Agers can be funny, humorous, and witty, but rarely joyous. A natural (or possibly *super*natural) mirth seems to escape them.

It occurred to me recently that there is something very unusual about New Age religion: there's no singing! Even though early Christianity's Gregorian-type chants were not the musical fare of our day, they were God-directed songs of praise, not repetitious expressions of self-worship. But in the New Age, you get none of the hymns of praise seen in the psalms, such as "come before him with joyful songs." Or "How good it is to sing praises to our God, how pleasant and fitting to praise him!" (Psalm 147:1). For that matter, you don't even get the psalms of the ancient Hindu vedas.

Nor do you hear the joyous singing of Miriam and the women of Israel when God delivered the nation from Egyptian bondage (Exodus 15:19-21). Or the mighty chorus celebrating the completion of the wall around Jerusalem, "rejoicing because God had given them great joy" (Nehemiah 12:27-43). Singing praise to ourselves because we are god somehow falls short of the whole idea. Maybe that's why there is no singing in the New Age. It's knowing that we have a great God of creation and salvation that makes Christians want to sing praises!

It's also a matter of having complete joy in Christ, to whom we are married as a radiant bride. It is inner peace expressing itself in outward praise. The apostle Paul contrasted the artificiality of what amounts to drinking songs with the spontaneity of singing which comes from one who is filled with the Holy Spirit:

> Do not get drunk on wine, which leads to debauchery. Instead, be filled with the Spirit. Speak to one another with psalms, hymns and spiritual songs. Sing and make music in your heart to the Lord, always giving thanks to God the Father for everything, in the name of our Lord Jesus Christ. (Ephesians 5:18-20)

Like alcohol-lubricated drinking songs, New Age chants and mantras are artificial forms of expression. They cannot bring one into contact with a god bigger than themselves. Their chants do not fill the earth with hymns of praise. They only echo off the walls of their own emptiness.

MUSIC OF THE GODS?

Should it be surprising, then, that New Age music is mostly instrumental, to accompany relaxation and meditation? Some have been so unkind as to call it "audio valium" or "yuppie Musak." I must confess that, given a choice, I much prefer New Age music to the hard rock that seems to dominate the radio waves. (Not that those are particularly great options, given the fact that much of New Age music is rather boring to my taste.)

On the other hand, at the risk of losing my credibility as a critic of the New Age movement, I must also confess that many of my all-night writing sessions are accompanied by one of my favorite pieces of music, George Winston's classic *December*, the first New Age record ever to go platinum. The Windham Hill label has produced some extremely good records, along with mountains of what many people consider to be almost "non-music." I should also point out that *December* contains overtly Christian content, centering as it does, on a month including Christmas. Again, we are challenged to discernment.

What I find interesting about most New Age music is the way in which it reflects the aimlessness and purposeless of the New Age message. Largely unstructured and circular in form, it resembles the *lawlessness* of New Age philosophy and the *reincarnational* theme of never-ending, repetitious life forms. Not surprisingly, then, New Age music often lacks resolution. And just as the line between right and wrong, good and evil, is blurred, so too we find a blurring of tones.

Beethoven noted the significant relationship between music and philosophy, observing that "music is the mediator between the life of the senses and the life of the spirit." Compare New Age music's typically monotone melodies (all is one?) with classical music's order and structured harmony, and you see in each a reflection of sharply contrasting world views.

One does not become a New Ager simply by listening to New Age music. But one can learn a lot about what New Agers are wanting us to believe by what we hear in their music. Do we really want a social fabric based on self-determined "lawlessness?" Can we live in a world where the difference between good and evil is a chalk line blown away by the capricious winds of moral relativism? Do we want a future without resolution, where Hitler and child abusers and those who callously pollute the environment are never brought to justice? This philosophy may be hitting today's pop charts, but it's not music to my ears.

SWEET DREAMS FOR A NEW AGE

One of the latest fads, in keeping with the New Age movement, is the emphasis on dreams and their interpretation. It has become quite the "in thing" to keep dream journals—records of one's dreams over a given period of time. You can even buy a computer program which allows you to store each dream for future reference. It comes complete with all the occult symbols said to be specially associated with dreams. When a sufficient number of the symbols reoccur, the computer displays the developing pattern for you and suggests the correct interpretation.

Based upon their dreams and the various innovative means of interpreting them, people are making some of the most important decisions of their lives, affecting even personal relationships, financial affairs, and questions of diet. One wonders how far removed these efforts at inner guidance may be from the "God-told-me" approach popular among Christians in recent times. Is one form of subjectivity more accurate than the other? Is either verifiable? Is it possible that both are means of justifying what we want to do in the first place?

The Bible does not rule out the possibility that God has spoken through dreams.

> For God does speak—now one way, now another—though man may not perceive it. In a dream, in a vision of the night, when deep sleep falls on men as they slumber in their beds, he may speak in their ears and terrify them with warnings, to turn man from wrongdoing and keep him from pride, to preserve his soul from the pit, his life from perishing by the sword. (Job 33:14-18)

At a time when there was no written revelation from God, such as we have been given through the Bible, dreams were simply one among several direct ways in which God revealed himself to man.

The surprising thing about such message-laden dreams is the number of them we find in the Bible. I count at least twenty specific dreams to people like Jacob, his son Joseph, Pharaoh, Gideon, Nebuchadnezzar, Mary's husband

Joseph, the wise men at Jesus' birth, and the wife of Pontius Pilate. Fully half of those dreams contained warnings from God about impending danger. Another half dozen or so brought good news, like the impending birth of Jesus! Dreams were a means by which God often spoke to the prophets, and Joel predicted a time when young men and women would dream dreams as a manifestation of God's power (Joel 2:28).

In most cases, the dreams had to be interpreted by someone else—a fact that led to widespread abuse by false prophets willing to invent dream interpretations for a price. When Pharaoh asked Joseph to interpret his dream, Joseph pointed to God as the interpreter: "'I cannot do it,' Joseph replied to Pharaoh, 'but God will give Pharaoh the answer he desires'" (Genesis 41:16).

A biblical test of proper dream interpretation in the early centuries calls into serious question any dream scheme promoted by the modern-day New Age movement:

> If a prophet, or one who foretells by dreams, appears among you and announces to you a miraculous sign or wonder, and if the sign or wonder of which he has spoken takes place, and he says, "Let us follow other gods" (gods you have not known) "and let us worship them," you must not listen to the words of that prophet or dreamer. The LORD your God is testing you to find out whether you love him with all your heart and with all your soul. It is the LORD your God you must follow, and him you must revere. Keep his commands and obey him; serve him and hold fast to him. (Deuteronomy 13:1-4)

Because the New Age movement leads us away from the Creator God of the Bible, we must not allow their many methods of dream interpretation to control our actions.

If there have been God-sent dreams in the past, the

biblical view of our nocturnal visions is less than encouraging for those who might wish to keep dream journals and seek deep meaning from their nightly musings. Our ordinary dreams are viewed as vanishing fantasies, the products of our own worried minds, and basically meaningless:

> As a dream when one awakes, so when you arise, O Lord, you will despise them as fantasies. (Psalm 73:20)
>
> As a dream comes when there are many cares, so the speech of a fool when there are many words. (Ecclesiastes 5:3)
>
> Much dreaming and many words are meaningless. Therefore stand in awe of God. (Ecclesiastes 5:7)

In light of the claim by some New Agers that what we dream is literally occurring at the moment of the dream sequence, one biblical passage is especially important:

> Then the hordes of all the nations that fight against Ariel, that attack her and her fortress and besiege her, will be as it is with a dream, with a vision in the night—as when a hungry man dreams that he is eating, but he awakens, and his hunger remains; as when a thirsty man dreams that he is drinking, but he awakens faint, with his thirst unquenched. (Isaiah 29:7, 8)

Certainly, but for the occasional coincidence, there does not appear to be a connection between our dreams and the reality of what they portray. Considering the occasional nightmare, it's a good thing! Of course, sleepwalkers may come closer to encountering the reality of their dreams. A cousin of mine, a notorious somnambulist, awoke from a dream about a rooster crowing to find himself perched on the foot of his bed, doing what observers declare was a pretty fair rendition of cock-a-doodle-do!

At the most, it could be said that we tend to dream about things that are weighing heavily on our minds in any event. It's as if everyone is gone from the office for the night except for a mail clerk in the back room, sorting out the next day's messages. Sometimes he gets them in all the right pigeon-holes; sometimes it seems that he goes raving mad. Personally, I rarely dream. But when I am in one of my "writing modes," I wake up frequently during the night with ideas that beg to be scribbled on the notepad which I keep handy on the night table. Some of my best "writing" comes when the brain is relaxed during sleep.

If we are not always sure of the significance of our dreams, there is one thing we *can* be sure of: our dreams will never be a message from God that would contradict what God already has told us in his revealed Word. Given a choice between dreams and God's Word, dreams don't come in first—or second. They don't even compete. The prophet Jeremiah put the comparison graphically:

> "Let the prophet who has a dream tell his dream, but let the one who has my word speak it faithfully. For what has straw to do with grain?" declares the LORD. (Jeremiah 23:28)

For Jeremiah, the only sure guide to our daily life is found in the words of Scripture. Unlike my dreams, which cause me to speculate and wonder whether I am correct, God's Word is "a lamp to my feet and a light for my path" (Psalm 119:105).

Dreams are to be enjoyed, shared, and made the objects of our intense curiosity. But they can only mislead and disappoint us as explanations, predictions, or sources of spiritual insight. Dream journals for fun and sheer interest? Why not? But discretion once again is the key. Dreams can be frightening enough. Who would want a life lived by one's dreams to turn into a nightmare?

DISCRETION, DISCRETION—ALWAYS DISCRETION

Today, the need for discretion is urgent. Crystal lies typically are half-truths. Virtually always, there is a residue of truth involved in the deception. Just enough to entice us. Just the right amount to confuse us. Just one step beyond where it seems safe.

A fascination with UFO's can be the stuff from which good sci-fi is made, until we are told that extraterrestrials inside those UFO's are bringing us new spiritual truths. Reading accounts of those who have "died" and come back is altogether intriguing, until someone suggests that these near-death experiences prove reincarnation. Experiencing *deja vu* is a delightfully curious phenomenon, until we are told that what we are seeing for "the second time" was seen "the first time" in one of our past lives. ESP (extrasensory perception) is a fascinating mystery, until it is offered as proof that we are entities in tune with the universal energy which is God.

To admit the reality of paranormal experiences is not to admit the philosophical New Age doctrines based upon them. Likewise, to deny the validity of New Age thought is not to deny the many unexplainable forces either in nature or within the spiritual dimension. The caution is this: *Some* explanation is not necessarily better than *no* explanation. Particularly this is true when the explanation that is given contradicts God's written revelation—even human experience and common sense.

Discernment. If only it could become the password of our time. And *biblical knowledge,* which it presupposes. As God said through the prophet Hosea, "My people are destroyed from lack of knowledge" (Hosea 4:6). In order to exercise discretion properly, we must familiarize ourselves with God's Word. In the New Age with which we are confronted, having only a superficial understanding of broad Christian themes will leave us vulnerable to spiritual counterfeits.

Knowledge, understanding, and prayerful discernment—these are our safeguards. When we are properly equipped, the deceptive practices of the crystal kingdom become crystal clear.

TEN

Healing and Holistic Health

O VER A PERIOD OF SEVERAL MONTHS NOW, a churchgoing neighbor of mine has found relief for her arthritic hand—so tightly frozen that she couldn't open it—through treatments she has been receiving from an acupuncturist. Another friend in a nearby village has been visiting his local acupuncturist, following a stroke which left him partially paralyzed and completely frustrated. He can't point to any specific progress yet, but believes he is being helped by the treatments. The purpose of acupuncture, he is told, is to unblock the invisible energy lines which run through his body.

His wife, on the other hand, went to a local Church of England rector when her shoulder wouldn't move. She went only to please someone else but found, to her amazement, that his mere gentle touch and quiet talk brought both an unusual sense of relaxation and a shoulder restored like new!

One of my students, a young woman from the Philippines, is quite convinced that psychic surgeons active in her part of the world are successful in removing cancers from unanesthetized persons, simply by reaching into the body and removing the mass of diseased tissue. She's not at all dissuaded by evidence suggesting magical sleight-of-hand.

More than a million people in Brazil, who received healings from an uneducated government clerk called simply "Arigo" (loosely translated *country bumpkin*) would agree with her. Defying all logic and known medical practices, Arigo would viciously plunge a knife into eye sockets, cut out tumors (stopping bleeding on command), or hastily scribble out prescriptions having no apparent relation to the patient's illness. Never charging for his services, Arigo healed over 300 people a day for two decades, spending perhaps no more than a minute with each. Arigo became so famous that even former Brazilian president Kubitschek sought his treatment.

Edgar Cayce, mentioned earlier as the father of the New Age movement, apparently was a successful psychic healer long before his psychic "readings" convinced him that the Bible had it all wrong and that Eastern mysticism was the true explanation of life. Knowing nothing more than the person's name and location, Cayce diagnosed illnesses and prescribed unlikely remedies while he was in a self-induced trance. Like Arigo, he rarely received payment and was never proved to be a fraud. Thousands of people in the early 1900s claimed healing through Cayce's readings.

Another of my students, a Christian Scientist, believes that disease is the product of one's limited, human perception. By her belief, disease can be "cured" through the intervention of a Christian Science practitioner who helps the "sick" person realize that the illness doesn't actually exist in the first place. Her skeptical fellow students in my Law and Religion class responded with piercing interrogation when she presented her paper, detailing this metaphysical—New Age-like—world view. Her defense was unswerving. However, she did give me a knowing laugh recently when I discovered her in the hallway in obvious agony. "Yep, it's a headache," she confessed with some embarrassment. Following on the heels of our discussion about her Christian Science beliefs, she was already anticipating my smug smile!

FAITH HEALINGS AND VITAMINS

A newly found friend of mine is an evangelist who travels frequently to Africa, India, and the Far East. As part of his crusades, he includes faith healing. He can't say how he does it, other than through faith and God's power, but he claims to have healed hundreds of people. According to him, the lame walk and the blind see. Although I believe in God's power to heal (otherwise why pray?), the lawyer in me wants to examine the case more closely. Are they the same kind of lame and blind (often from birth) that Jesus and the apostles healed? Or are there alternative explanations involved?

Other Christian friends, who pray for the healthy recovery of those they love, have not always had their prayers answered—at least result-wise. Like you, I have prayed many times for God to heal someone who was facing death or disease, only to learn of their passing away without the recovery I had wanted so desperately. Perhaps that is why, like Jesus, we pray "Thy will be done."

Alternative medicine is not something new in my life. I grew up in a home where castor oil and other home remedies were the order of the day, and where there were frequent trips to chiropractors and homeopathic doctors, who reject the use of drugs and work through "natural" cures. Our refrigerator contained jars of homemade yogurt before yogurt became popular (and before it became half-way edible, thanks to the addition of fruits and flavoring). The bottle of sulfur water over in the corner was the next best remedy for whatever ails you, second only to Hadacol (which later was exposed as being about 98% alcohol!).

To this day, my mother's favorite periodical is *Prevention Magazine,* the layman's guide to natural health and diet. And her vast array of vitamins is supposed to cure virtually every health problem known to man. What megadoses of vitamins won't cure, barley green will. (If you don't know about barley green, don't ask!) Unlike my mother, my dad never went in for this "bunch of foolishness." Dad's gone now. Who knows whether greater openness to less orthodox approaches to good health might have increased the length of his life?

WHAT'S THE TRUTH ABOUT HEALING?

In view of this litany of conflicting views, I'm not sure I understand all that I know about medicine, therapy, and healing, apart from my firm belief from Scripture that God can heal miraculously. And, further, that my prayers can initiate, although never demand, his act of healing. I do know that medical science extended my life beyond its 22nd year. Without surgery and modern post operative care, I likely would have died from an appendix which had ruptured a month before it was discovered. As it was, it was somewhat of a close call.

Yet I also believe that I was instrumental in curing a serious case of ulcers in my younger years. I suppose you could call it mind over matter. A prescribed bland diet undoubtedly contributed far less to the cure than my intentional change in lifestyle. Almost overnight, I abandoned a rather driven, "Type A" personality and "mellowed out." Maybe it *was* the diet. Maybe it was sheer coincidence. But my money is on mind over matter—a change of outlook, a new perspective.

By some coincidence, just yesterday I experienced another healing. Two days before, using my right leg, I stepped down hard on a long piece of wood that I was holding at an angle in my left hand. The idea was to break the piece of wood in two. When the wood finally gave way to the pressure, so did my right knee. I soon found that I could barely walk, and by no means could I descend the stairs. For two days, I gave the knee a rest, trying not to walk on it at all. Yesterday, I thought it might be best to give it a cautious workout.

With a walking stick in hand, I dragged myself out of the cottage and onto the narrow wooded equestrian trail leading to the next village. Limping like an old man, I plodded my way ever so slowly to an open pasture which led up the hill. Walking uphill seemed a little less painful, but I was clearly in trouble. It was time to see the doctor, I decided. Having managed to reach a trail back towards the village, I climbed carefully over a fence into another pasture where five black cows curiously noted my bent frame and tentative gait. They followed after me slowly in single file— something they had never done before—as if to share my pain.

I soon became lost in thought. Then, all of a sudden, I heard the sound of cows running towards me. I turned around to see the cows rapidly bearing down on me, as if to say "Enough of this limping stuff, let's run for awhile!" Seeing me stand my ground in front of them, they skidded to a halt and then began playfully butting heads with each other. As I turned back around and started to walk away, I realized that I could walk again! First one step and then another. Even downhill. There was some residual pain, but I could tell the knee was working properly again. "Let this story get out," I chuckled to myself, "and my little village will become another Lourdes."

Yesterday's experience caused me to reflect on this chapter, which I was about to write on the holistic healing promoted by the New Age movement. What if I had gone to an acupuncturist the day before? Or been diagnosed by iridology? Suppose someone had suggested opening up my chakras, and that I had sat for hours in silent, serious meditation in order to achieve that? Indeed, what if I had been *visualizing* a well knee when the cure took place? Would not I have attributed my cure to each of these methods?

Normally we do tend to associate "healing" with whatever method of treatment we have applied to the problem. Yet, in this case, I am sure that the external circumstances of the healing of my knee were only coincidental. I probably turned at just the right angle to pop my knee back into place. Could it be that other "healings" result coincidentally along with medical or holistic treatment?

HEALING HOLISTICALLY

In the New Age movement, holistic healing is based on a belief that the human body is more than a physical specimen to be poked, pulled, and put under the knife. The idea of "holism" is to see the human *body* as part of a human *being*. For that, the New Age movement is to be greatly commended. Such a perspective is long overdue by a medical profession that sometimes looks more like an assembly line, an insurance company, and a pharmaceutical house all rolled into one!

The bad news is that although holistic medicine recognizes a spiritual dimension to human beings, it fails to account for a *supernatural* dimension in which a God outside of ourselves operates. More bad news is that the reality of disease and death is virtually denied, being viewed as merely illusory (begging the question of why *any* physical treatment is employed). And the worst news of all is that holistic medicine's world view, for the most part, is a pagan denial of the God of creation. The goal of holistic healing is not simply to reform the medical profession, but to reshape our thinking toward New Age paganism.

Acupuncture, for example, is an ancient Chinese form of

treatment which assumes the flow of universal (all is one) energy, known as Ch'i, throughout the body. This Taoist concept, in which the universal energy is God, is also the foundation for acupressure, preferred by many who shrink back at the thought of needles being put under their skin in acupuncture. The purpose of each method is to unblock the universal energy by disturbing various points in the body which act like gates to open and close the flow of energy.

Almost by definition, there is no verifiable evidence of the twelve invisible channels known as *meridians.* Nor is there convincing evidence to indicate that the meridians' supposed relationship to the body's organs is sound physiology. To the extent that acupuncture helps to relieve pain, it may be based as much upon the patient's expectations as upon the treatment itself.

Perhaps the most important thing about acupuncture is that virtually all acupuncturists, despite occasionally wearing "Christian" labels, are adherents of Eastern or New Age thinking. Acupuncture and acupressure are methods of healing consistent with a belief system wholly foreign to Scripture. This is not to say that their methods cannot bring about successful results in some cases. It simply stands as a warning against being enticed by the *philosophy* which gave birth to the *practice.*

The practice of "therapeutic touch" is but an updated version of the same basic Taoist and Hindu concept of universal energy. Thousands of nurses have been trained to locate a patient's blockage or congestion by scanning the body's "energy field" with their hands. Having done that, the nurse is instructed to transfer his or her own energy to the patient, visualizing and creating the desired result and passing it along through the hands to the patient. Such touching is sometimes associated with colors, each color having a different desired effect.

It is one thing to appreciate the healing value of a warm, caring touch, as when a mother instinctively strokes the fevered brow of her child. It is quite another thing to propose

(a) that there is a universal energy which happens to be God and (b) that we can be a conduit for that energy in bringing about another's healing. In such a case, mystical is magical.

The farther you get into New Age healing, the closer you come to Eastern religion. Involvement with mystical chakras, yin and yang, "centering," and the five elements of Taoism takes you from the threshold of healing into the inner sanctuary of pagan presuppositions. The road of holistic healing can easily lead from methods associated with universal energy to a belief that all is one, to the affirmation that we are God.

The road to enlightenment also happens to lead backwards to ancient superstition and pagan idolatry. It is said that crystals have the power to heal and that universal energy can be intensified through pyramid power. In trendy Southern California, upper-middle-class residents of suburban communities park their Mercedes-Benzes, enter the back room of their local New Age bookstore, sit in the lotus position under a giant tubular pyramid, and meditate while gazing at an altar of colored crystals at the front of the room. Or on the way out they can buy "healing crystals," advertised as cures for a wide variety of ailments.

There is absolutely no credible evidence to support healing by crystals. One wonders how much of the New Age hype is supplied by those who stand to profit from the sale of crystals. Prices of crystals have become astronomical. The New Age is far from metaphysical earthly detachment. New Age is big business. When it comes to crystal lies, the claimed healing qualities of crystals themselves must be right at the top of the list of New Age deception. Crystals are as faddish and commercial as the infamous pet rocks, and not a grain more therapeutic.

Other longstanding healing practices are now often adopted—and sometimes adapted—by the New Age movement. These include iridology (diagnosing ailments by looking at the eyes), homeopathy (drugless therapy), and biofeedback (controlling body functions using electronic monitoring equipment). Of these three, only biofeedback appears to have any medical legitimacy. Add to these three purported healing methods a growing interest in New Age philosophy among many chiropractors, and you start to see the wide influence of New Age thinking.

As in the last chapter, the operative word with New Age and Eastern healing practices is *discernment*. Anyone wishing to learn more about these practices should pick up a copy of *New Age Medicine* (Global Publishers) by Paul C. Reisser, M.D., Teri K. Reisser, and John Weldon. It contains a well-balanced, informed review of holistic healing in the New Age. In addition to the practices mentioned in this chapter, the authors discuss kinesiology (muscle testing), orgonomy, yoga, zone therapy, reflexology, Rolfing, Do'in, Shiatsu, Polar therapy, and bioenergetic analysis.

Whatever the latest (or most ancient) practice, we must be careful to recognize that simply because a healing method *works* is no guarantee that it is safe spiritually. In *Out On a Broken Limb,* I documented at length the readings given by Edgar Cayce regarding his own supposed past lives and those of Jesus. If his psychic healings were not proved to be fraudulent, his hundreds of New Age "life readings" cannot escape the charge. They are both fraudulent and blasphemous. This leads one to question whether people like Cayce and Brazil's Arigo are not unwitting pawns in Satan's campaign to deceive us. With Cayce, in particular, the *message* brought by "the sleeping prophet" was clearly demonic. Were his seemingly legitimate healings simply hors d'oeuvres for a main course of crystal lies?

JESUS' MIRACULOUS HEALINGS

In contrast to holistic healing in the New Age, we see quite a different picture in the healings done by Jesus and his apostles. It would be easy enough to dismiss holistic healing by pointing out that Jesus never employed any of the Eastern or New Age methods, whether acupuncture, acupressure, or iridology. Nowhere is there any indication that he encouraged his disciples to use yoga, meditation, or visualization. Nor did he perform psychic surgery or employ the use of spirit guides. All of that is completely foreign to the miracles he performed.

Then again, neither did Jesus prescribe pills or perform modern Western-style medical surgery. His healings were neither the practice of medical science nor mind over matter. They were achieved miraculously through the power of God. He did not promise that everyone had equal access to this healing power, whether as a healer or as one to be healed.

Nor did he heal every diseased or handicapped person with whom he came into contact. Healing was not the central purpose of his ministry. Spiritual salvation was the reason for his appearance on the earth. His healings sometimes were motivated by sheer compassion, as in the case of the widow's dead son. ("When the Lord saw her, his heart went out to her and he said, 'Don't cry,'" Luke 7:13.) But principally the miracles were intended as confirmation of his claim to be God in the flesh, and of his message of salvation. ("'Unless you people see miraculous signs and wonders . . . you will never believe,'" John 4:48.)

Of the scores, perhaps hundreds, of Jesus' healings for which no further details are given, the gospel accounts record at least twenty-two specific healings. In those instances, Jesus healed people of more than a dozen different diseases or physical impairments. He also brought three people back to life after they already had died. Where much of New Age healing requires therapeutic touching, massage, pricking, or pressure, at least three of Jesus' healings were accomplished when he was at great distance from those who were near death. At the moment he commanded the healing, the sick person, in another location altogether, was healed.

On occasion, Jesus did physically touch those whom he healed. And twice, he spat on them or applied a compact of mud and saliva! But in six of the specific instances we are given, Jesus merely spoke a healing command, and the healing was accomplished. In one of the most telling instances, a woman was healed when she simply reached out and touched Jesus' clothes as he walked by (Mark 5:24-34). For her, it wasn't a matter of meridians and chakras or altered consciousness. It was simple faith in the power of God to heal. ("Daughter, your faith has healed you. Go in peace and be freed from your suffering," Mark 5:34.)

Surprisingly, however, the faith of the one being healed figured into only a handful of the other recorded healings. The faith of the healer was far more important in the case of the apostles themselves. When they were unable to heal a young boy of epileptic seizures, they questioned Jesus about it:

> Then the disciples came to Jesus in private and asked, "Why couldn't we drive it out?" He replied, "Because you have so little faith. I tell you the truth, if you have faith as small as a mustard seed, you can say to this mountain, 'Move from here to there' and it will move. Nothing will be impossible for you." (Matthew 17:19, 20)

Mark's account of the same incident notes one additional ingredient for the success of their healings: "He replied, 'This kind can come out only by prayer'" (Mark 9:29). Once again, we find a distinct difference between biblical healing and holistic healing. Biblical healing was based upon faith, prayer, and the supernatural healing power of the God of creation.

New Age healing uses clever plays on words to minimize the reality of sickness. *Disease,* we are told, is nothing more than *dis-ease* caused by not being in tune with the energy forces of the universe, being "out of balance" with the harmony of nature, or failing to recognize our own divinity. Healing comes about through *at-one-ment* with the "isness" of one's self—a terribly cheap imitation of the spiritual *atonement* for which Christ died on the cross. If Jesus did not heal everyone with whom he came into contact, at least he did not try to mislead them into thinking they *had* no disease, pain, or suffering—that it was all in their minds.

HEALING BY THE APOSTLES

Peter, Paul, and the other apostles also performed many healings, of which at least six are specifically recorded for us. Twice, they even brought people back from death to life. Like Jesus, they spoke the healing into being on half of those occasions and combined the command to heal with some form of touching in the other half. Jesus had said that, among the signs which would accompany the disciples as they went out to teach and baptize the nations, would be that: "They will place their hands on sick people, and they will get well" (Mark 16:18). "Laying on of hands," yes, but you never find the apostles using New Age-type massage or so-called "Therapeutic Touching."

In the case of those who were already dead, in particular, we see that the faith of the recipient was not always a factor. What *did* seem to be a factor was the exercise of healing power in the name of Jesus. ("In the name of Jesus Christ of Nazareth, walk," Acts 3:6.)That factor in healing would certainly not suit today's New Agers, who deny Jesus' lordship and advocate self-healing through mind over matter.

Rather than healings, one wonders if New Agers haven't brought about their own blindness. There was at least one occasion where a sorcerer in the mold of today's New Age mediums and channelers found Paul's miraculous power to heal turned into a nightmare of literal blindness. The warning contained in the incident is worthwhile reading for anyone engaged in misleading the public about God's truth:

> They traveled through the whole island until they came to Paphos. There they met a Jewish sorcerer and false prophet named Bar-Jesus, who was an attendant of the proconsul, Sergius Paulus. The proconsul, an intelligent man, sent for Barnabas and Saul because he wanted to hear the word of God. But Elymas the sorcerer (for that is what his name means) opposed them and tried to turn the proconsul from the faith. Then Saul, who was also called Paul, filled with the Holy Spirit, looked straight at Elymas and said, "You are a child of the devil and an enemy of everything that is right! You are full of all kinds of deceit and trickery. Will you never stop perverting the right ways of the Lord? Now the hand of the Lord is against you. You are going to be blind, and for a time you will be unable to see the light of the sun."
>
> Immediately mist and darkness came over him, and he groped about, seeking someone to lead him by the hand. When the proconsul saw what had happened, he believed, for he was amazed at the teaching about the Lord. (Acts 13:6-12)

Where holistic medicine is just a front for false teaching about God, those who practice such deceit might well give serious consideration to the spiritual jeopardy in which they have placed themselves. If God has the power to heal, he also has the power to destroy.

SIN AND SICKNESS

The most intriguing passage of all regarding healing comes in the Epistle of James:

> Is any one of you in trouble? He should pray. Is anyone happy? Let him sing songs of praise. Is any one of you sick? He should call the elders of the church to pray over him and anoint him with oil in the name of the Lord. And the prayer offered in faith will make the sick person well; the Lord will raise him up. If he has sinned, he will be forgiven. Therefore confess your sins to each other and pray for each other so that you may be healed. The prayer of a righteous man is powerful and effective. (James 5:13-16)

More questions are raised by this passage than easy answers are found. Why, for example, are the elders being called to the ministry of healing? What role does the anointing of oil have in the healing process? Is it somehow different from the "laying on of hands" which Jesus said would be involved in the healing process? Indeed, is there one method for nonbelievers being evangelized, and one for Christians in fellowship with a local congregation?

Perhaps most intriguing of all—is there a relationship between physical disease and sin, as seems to be suggested? Or is the "sickness" described here actually referring solely to spiritual sickness, as some have suggested? It is interesting to note that Jesus' healing of the paralytic who was let down through the roof of a house by his friends also seems to tie together sin and sickness:

> When Jesus saw their faith, he said to the paralytic, "Son, your sins are forgiven."
> "Which is easier: to say to the paralytic, 'Your sins are forgiven,' or to say, 'Get up, take your mat and walk'? But

that you may know that the Son of Man has authority on earth to forgive sins. . . ." He said to the paralytic, "I tell you, get up, take your mat and go home." He got up, took his mat and walked out in full view of them all. This amazed everyone and they praised God, saying, "We have never seen anything like this!" (Mark 2:5, 9-12)

But this may not be the end of the matter. If there is any lesson we ought to learn from the Book of Job, it is the message that there is not necessarily a connection between sickness and sin. Certainly, nowhere in Scripture do we see a kind of karmic causal relationship between the two. If sin can bring disease—as in the case of drinking and delirium tremens or illicit sex and AIDS—not all disease is the result of sin. A person doesn't get cancer from cheating on his taxes or break his leg because he has committed adultery.

There are two obscure hints in the apostle Paul's writings that would also disassociate sin from sickness. One is where he tells his young protege Timothy, "Stop drinking only water, and use a little wine because of your stomach and your frequent illnesses" (1 Timothy 5:23). The other is where, in passing, he notes, "I left Trophimus sick in Miletus" (2 Timothy 4:20). In neither case does he imply that they were sick because of some moral or spiritual defect. He assumes natural causes.

Perhaps most surprising is the fact that Paul, who had the power to heal, did not use that power for two of his closest associates! Nor is it written that he told them to call for local elders to come and anoint them with oil, as James had directed. To Timothy, Paul gives what might amount to a home remedy, a remedy we might even question in terms of its potential for medicinal effectiveness. And, clearest of all, Paul did not suggest that their illness was a figment of their imagination or the result of energy blockage or the lack of "centering" or any other such New Age explanations. Paul took their illness at face value and, for Timothy, took an approach more consistent with medical science than with metaphysics.

And yet when Jesus and James comfortably refer to sin and sickness in the same breath, we may be close to that part of holistic health which contains great truth. New Agers are correct in telling secular humanists that we are more than flesh and blood, more than molecules and subatomic particles which biologically have evolved into the human body. We are also spiritual beings. We have souls. And the relationship between mind, body, and soul is not just coincidental. We are mind, body, and soul intermingled. What we do in our bodies affects the soul, and our state of mind impacts heavily our physical condition.

To fully appreciate that interconnectedness, all we have to do is think about the body language we see everywhere around us. If someone is depressed, we recognize his condition by his lowered head, sad face, and listless movements. If someone is excited beyond containment, she is a blur of physical activity, with head high and a skip in her walk. We also know that when older people give up on life, it isn't long before they are dead. And Norman Cousins, who immersed himself in humor to overcome what should have been a terminal illness, advocates a strong case for laughter being the best medicine.

The "placebo effect," where people are given some inactive substance to make them think they are receiving curative medicine, is well documented. If they *think* they are healed, then they *are* healed! The same psychological deception can also be the explanation for many "faith healings" claimed by Christian faith healers, particularly where the illness is psychosomatic.

Therefore, holistic medicine must not be a reactionary baby thrown out with the New Age bath water. For too long, we have been brainwashed into thinking that pills cure all and that the medical profession is just a step below God. Our drug culture is hooked not just on heroin and cocaine. It's also hooked on the widespread respectability of aspirin and Valium. And even a drug-addicted medical system has not always met with success, despite the "medical miracles" which sometimes lull us into believing medicine's infallibility.

Many people will testify that modern medicine has taken their money, but done little for their health. In that respect, perhaps nothing has changed from the time of Jesus. Remember that line regarding the woman who reached out to touch the hem of Jesus' garment: "She had suffered a great deal under the care of many doctors and had spent all she had, yet instead of getting better she grew worse" (Mark 5:26).

HOLISTIC OR WHOLENESS?

When Jesus healed the paralytic (Mark, chapter 2), he did not stop there. He was far more concerned about the man's soul. It is altogether possible that healing of the paralysis might have been accomplished by modern medical science, but forgiving the man his sins could only be done by God. It suggests two important points. First, holistic health has the right idea if what it points to is the need for *wholistic* health in which we regard man as mind, body, *and* soul. In which we look to those mental, emotional, even spiritual problems, which affect a person's health. Where we seek a three-dimensional view of the patient. In this, the New Age movement is right. Looking at people as a *whole* is more likely to solve the *whole* problem.

Yet what New Agers must come to understand is that sin is also part of man's wholeness, or rather his *lack* of being whole. The New Age practitioner who disregards the reality of sin is as blind to wholeness as the medical doctor who sees the body only as a chemical and electrical mass to be repaired like a broken computer or automobile. It's no use talking about holism until we understand holiness. In fact, holism and holiness come from a common linguistic root.

A person can be shriveled, broken, and diseased, yet *whole* in God's sight. Another person can be as healthy as a horse, yet spiritually dead. When God says, "Choose life," he is looking to a life of righteousness, not simply a life of good physical health. For, "What good will it be for a man if he gains the whole world, yet forfeits his soul?" (Matthew 16:26). Disease is not our greatest enemy, nor even death. Sin is our greatest enemy, and spiritual death our worst destiny.

As the greatest of all psychological deceptions, New Age philosophy inevitably will fail at being more than a spiritual placebo. The Great Physician is the one in whom we must place our trust for true wholeness. It is in him that we are complete. Not only is he the Way and the Truth, he is also the Life.

ELEVEN

Deadly Deception

S INCE WRITING *Out On a Broken Limb,* I have received
hundreds of letters, some disapproving, but many more
expressing gratitude for exposing the dangers in the New
Age movement. Typical was this week's mail. On the same
day, I received two letters. The first, from Oskaloosa, Iowa,
criticized me for being critical of Shirley MacLaine. "Just
being a negative critic isn't going to do a lot of good," said
the writer. And, of course, he is right about that, although I
cringe at the thought that anyone could have read my book
and not found positive, biblical encouragement in it as well.

More typical of the responses in the letter box is this one
from Lakewood, Colorado:

Dear Dr. Smith,
I am writing to thank you for writing your book *Out On a
Broken Limb.* I read the book almost two years ago and it
was crucial in leading me to Christ. I was confused by
your book initially because I was not ready to accept that
Christ is THE way, THE truth, and THE life, however,
your book convinced me that my New Age beliefs could
not be enmeshed with the nominal Christian background
I grew up with. I am now a Christian of almost a year and I
am thinking of spending my life in some type of ministry,

possibly becoming a missionary to the Far East, God willing, after I graduate from Colorado State University. I thank you and praise God that you spent the time and effort in writing a book that has helped my life turn to one focused on Jesus Christ and the message of Truth and Good News He gave to us in love.

I share this letter with you to emphasize the seriousness of the subject we are discussing. This letter could have been multiplied by scores of others, telling of lives once headed into the deadly deception of the New Age but retrieved when the crystal lies of the New Age were exposed to the light of God's Word. We are not involved here in merely a philosophical discussion where everyone enjoys arguing with each other, then goes home. It is not simply a matter of criticizing Shirley MacLaine, J. Z. Knight, or anyone else caught up in the movement. Nor is it simply a fundamentalist reaction to supposedly more enlightened thinking. The New Age movement is shattering lives, marriages, and families.

Some time ago, a young man whom I know started reading New Age literature. It wasn't long before he quit going to church, told his wife he was leaving her, and began living with another woman—a New Ager like himself. His explanation? "New Age has given me a sense of freedom. I see things in a totally different light now." What great truth had he learned from the New Age? Apparently, that he could leave his lovely wife for another woman! Is that the enlightenment to which the New Age calls us?

Recently, during our worship, a man sitting in front of me at church turned around and handed me a note scrawled on the back of the church bulletin. Here was a man who had reached the pinnacle of influence in his profession, yet in his note he was begging me for answers to a problem which completely mystified him. His wife of many years had recently written him a letter saying that she was leaving him. The reason? "I have been reading books by Shirley MacLaine and others who have shown me a new truth about who I am and my power to choose who I want to be. And I am choosing to leave you." Certainly no one is going to say that their marriage failed because of Shirley MacLaine. Surely, there were ongoing problems in the marriage, hidden somewhere beneath the surface. But the "easy out" was consistent with New Age teaching. In the New Age, there is always an "easy out," whether it be from marriage, job stability, or even life itself.

NOT JUST ABSTRACT PHILOSOPHY

It bears repeating: Ideas have consequences. What we believe affects our lives. It changes who we are and how we act. It can build bridges of understanding, trust, and love, or destroy everything we've ever worked for. The New Age movement has all the right words—love, peace, brotherhood, and positive thinking. It *sounds* right: "Take control of your life." "Be responsible for yourself." "Visualize world peace." But I don't see it leading to happiness—or to lasting peace.

In the New Age movement, "Love your neighbor as yourself" becomes, "Choose your own good." Adultery, for example, is always given some cosmic explanation, involving one's right to choose such a relationship. We don't hear concern expressed for the spouse who is cheated on or left altogether for someone else. (Shirley MacLaine was even angry at the wife of the man with whom she was having an affair. "Why doesn't she let him go?" Ms. MacLaine fairly shouted!) Hardly ever do we see a call for moral responsibility. We can only ask whose life can be enhanced by a belief system which routinely calls for lawless self-direction?

If we are wrong about a scientific explanation for gravity,

it hardly matters. Our lives go on as usual. The same is true of our political beliefs. They rarely change who we are. But our religious or philosophical beliefs can dramatically affect the person we are inside and the way we act toward others outside. Thinking we are God—*saying* that we are God— cannot help but change who we are and how we relate to others. That's why we can ill afford to take lightly the deception of the New Age. In my files are letters upon letters testifying to the very real threat of New Age thinking. And, happily, to the renewal of lives brought back to Christ.

WHY PEOPLE BELIEVE IN THE NEW AGE

I continue to be amazed at how easily people can be led into the New Age movement. But its contagious appeal can't be denied. And over the past two years, I have observed some distinct categories to which New Age thinking has its greatest appeal. One group in particular, ex-Catholics, seem to head the list. The best illustration came on a recent *Donahue* show. A panel of five guests, including a popular actress and a former astronaut, were extolling the virtues of the New Age, when Phil Donahue asked: "What were you people religiously before you became interested in the New Age movement?" The replies came down the row with increasing impact: "Catholic." "Catholic." "Catholic." "Catholic." "Catholic." Donahue quickly added, "Me, too. The church has really done us wrong!" Read New Age literature even superficially and you will encounter acrid anti-church bitterness.

The New Age movement is not an exclusive fraternity for lapsed Catholics. There are many ex-Baptists (notably Shirley MacLaine and Edgar Cayce) and thousands from other Protestant backgrounds among the ranks of New Agers. But substantial numbers of those who have left the Roman Catholic Church for whatever reasons personal to themselves, are now turning to the New Age movement. They seem to be drawn by the lack of tradition, institutionalism, authority, and ritual. Of course, the moral guilt that so many New Agers are trying to escape is a point to be taken up with God, not the church.

If some church has turned you off, my advice is to take the focus off the church itself. Begin putting your focus on Jesus Christ, who is your Savior. Human beings make mistakes, but Jesus does not. Christ established his church as a family of Christians from whom we can draw mutual support and to whom we can give mutual encouragement. He calls us into an organism of faith, not into an organization of humanly-ordained rules.

We have already mentioned another group which has been drawn easily into the New Age movement: today's secular Jews. Not only does the New Age movement supply them with a belief in the afterlife, but it allows them to accept Jesus Christ as a great teacher, without ever having to become a Christian. For secular Jews, the New Age movement is the best of all worlds. But in turning from secularism to the New Age, they have traded one lie for another. If only they could see the advantage of a one-time resurrection over multiple incarnations into a world of suffering and sin and come to appreciate the beauty of Christ as Lord!

Women represent yet another distinct group especially attracted to the New Age movement. In a way, this should not come as a surprise. Women seem to be more spiritually oriented than men wherever we turn. But the percentage of New Age adherents who are women is particularly high—in the neighborhood of seventy-five to ninety percent. In *Men of Strength For Women of God* (Harvest House Publishers, 1989), I have discussed the New Age gender factor in far greater detail than is possible within the scope of this book. Suffice it to say here that the New Age movement and feminism go hand in hand.

I also suggest for your reading Russell Chandler's chapter

entitled "Goddesses and Neopagans" in *Understanding the New Age* (Word Publishing, 1988). Just one quotation will set the scene:

> Nature-based religion, particularly that of the [Great] Goddess and of Wicca (or "witchcraft"), is strong within the New Age strand often referred to as "ecofeminism." This feminist spirituality began to flower during the radical cultural movement of the 1970s. It views men as brutalizing women through sexual violence and porno-graphic exploitation, and dominating them through a stern, overbearing, male "skygod." (p. 121)

Add to this a special emphasis on *Mother*-Earth, such high priestesses of the movement as Shirley MacLaine and J.Z. Knight, an aversion to the "maleness" of the God of the Bible, and frequent references to God, using the pronoun *she,* and you begin to appreciate why so many women are attracted to the New Age. Perhaps the most telling feature of the movement is its appeal to right-brain, intuitive, *feminine* thinking, as opposed to left-brain, rational, *masculine* thinking.

The New Age movement also appeals to all those people who are trying desperately to escape the suffocating mater-ialism of our age. Even the embarrassing materialism of the church reminds them of the materialism of the world that is driving them desperately toward a spiritual quest. To those who seek something more sublime, the New Age movement promises a spiritual aspect to human existence and a spiritual solution to world peace, the environment, and other social issues. Unfortunately, the spiritual nature of the New Age movement is matched only by its commercialism. New Age is but another frustrating shopping center for those chasing the dream of true spirituality.

WHOLENESS IS IN CHRIST

Whatever one's reason for being attracted to the New Age movement, the allure is fool's gold. Personal fulfillment, inner joy, and lasting relationships are put at great risk. The apostle Paul put the warning this way:

> See to it that no one takes you captive through hollow and deceptive philosophy, which depends on human tradition and the basic principles of this world rather than on Christ. For in Christ all the fullness of the Deity lives in bodily form, and you have been given fullness in Christ, who is the head over every power and authority. (Colossians 2:8-10)

If it is fullness that we want, we will find it only in Christ. If it is wholeness that we desire, it too comes only through faith in the God of creation.

King Solomon, in his *Ecclesiastes,* looked around him at all the world had to offer: popularity, power, wealth—even wisdom. He realized that what life has to offer is as transitory as life itself. We can't take any of them with us when we die. And if you were to ask him, Solomon would tell you that coming back into this world again is sheer fantasy. Here's how he concluded his reflections on the meaning of life:

> Now all has been heard; here is the conclusion of the matter: Fear God and keep his commandments, for this is the whole duty of man. For God will bring every deed into judgment, including every hidden thing, whether it is good or evil. (Ecclesiastes 12:13, 14)

For those who seek a holistic world view, Solomon points us to the God of the Bible and to his teachings which it contains. In fact, the original language says simply: "Fear God and keep his commandments for this is the *whole* of man." *Wholeness* comes in submitting our lives to the leading of the One who has made us, and who therefore knows how we best function. *Wholeness* comes through *holiness* before God.

It is understandable that many people would want to forego having such wholeness if it means having to subject ourselves to God's judgment. Given a choice, who among us would really want to have everything about us exposed, "including every hidden thing, whether it is good or evil?" But the good news of Jesus Christ is that God has offered us grace to cover all our sins. In Christ, we do not stand naked before God. We are clothed in the righteousness of Christ! Clean. Pure. Justified.

If we are true seekers of human perfection, what more could we want? God offers to *deem* us perfect in one lifetime! If it is enlightenment we covet, how much clearer could life's meaning be? If it is truth that we value, why should we ever fall for glitzy, trendy deception? Compared with the genuine Truth of God, the crystal lies of the New Age movement are worthless baubles.

MAKING HARD CHOICES

The New Agers are right about one thing: we do have the responsibility for choosing what we believe. And between Christianity and New Age belief, the choices are clear:

• Are you and I really God, or is there a God of creation outside of ourselves? Can we really believe that we created ourselves and the universe around us?

• Are we divine beings with unlimited power over our circumstances, or are we finite mortals, created in the image of God? To whom will we turn when we have done all that we can do and still have failed?

• Is everything *one* or is there a distinction between God and man, between energy and matter, between the spiritual and the physical? Surely we are different from toads, frogs, clouds, and peanut butter!

• Is there really no difference between good and evil? Or, in fact, are we not caught in a constant struggle between the two? Are we really to believe that there is no evil in the world of human cruelty that invades our living rooms each evening on the six o'clock news?

• Are there no victims? Are we really to believe that we choose all the bad things that happen to us? Can we comfortably tell those who are less fortunate than ourselves that they have *chosen* their suffering?

• Is life nothing more than an illusion? Or is there a reality in which we live daily and eventually die? If it is an illusion, why do we *act* in every way as if it were real?

• Is there really no ultimate Truth? Or is there, in fact, a clear-cut line between right and wrong? Even denying the existence of ultimate Truth assumes the opposite conclusion to be true!

• Do we have many lifetimes to live, or is the Bible correct when it tells us that we live only once? If many lifetimes, why don't we remember them? What good does it do if we can't remember them?

• How are we to regard Jesus of Nazareth? Is he our Savior and Christ, the one and only Son of God, or was he just a great teacher who achieved Christ-consciousness, just as you and I can achieve? His miracles surely set him apart from ourselves and every other person who has ever lived. If his miraculous power is unmatched, his teaching is sublime!

• Is there no judgment to face after this life, or will our choices actually make a difference to our eternal destiny? If we are wrong, it will be too late to do anything about it.

ETERNAL LIFE IN THE BALANCE

The choices we make today will not be reversible after we die. There are no second chances in the next life. And for all the talk of life's being an illusion, there is one reality that none of us can escape. Death awaits us all. Death is the ultimate reality in this dimension. Faith in Jesus Christ and obedience to the will of God can take us safely into the world beyond and fulfill us in the life we have even now. The promises of the New Age movement are Satan's campaign rhetoric. But he is the Father of Lies. Crystal lies.

In the spirit of the New Age movement, there is much about which to be positive. In Jesus Christ there is life, and life abundantly! Just look at the great affirmations about life in Christ, as found in John's Gospel:

I have come that they may have life, and have it to the full. (John 10:10)

Then Jesus declared, "I am the bread of life. He who comes to me will never go hungry, and he who believes in me will never be thirsty." (John 6:35)

"Whoever drinks the water I give him will never thirst. Indeed, the water I give him will become in him a spring of water welling up to eternal life." (John 4:14)

"I tell you the truth, whoever hears my word and believes him who sent me has eternal life and will not be condemned; he has crossed over from death to life." (John 5:24)

"The Spirit gives life; the flesh counts for nothing. The words I have spoken to you are spirit and they are life." (John 6:63)

Simon Peter answered him, "Lord, to whom shall we go? You have the words of eternal life." (John 6:68)

Jesus answered, "I am the way and the truth and the life. No one comes to the Father except through me." (John 14:6)

Jesus said to her, "I am the resurrection and the life. He who believes in me will live, even though he dies; and whoever lives and believes in me will never die. Do you believe this?" (John 11:25, 26)

Jesus Christ: Life to the full here and now; life without death in the world to come. What more could we ask? What more could we want?

The apostle Paul reminds us of our assurance—the resurrection of Jesus Christ from the dead:

And if the Spirit of him who raised Jesus from the dead is living in you, he who raised Christ from the dead will also give life to your mortal bodies through his Spirit, who lives in you. (Romans 8:11)

Reincarnation is an unproved theory. Resurrection is historical fact. Which would you rather trust as the basis for your happiness and fulfillment?

And where is the love of God in the New Age? Is it in the love of self? If so, where will that love be after we're gone? With the apostle Paul, I choose to believe in a God whose love sustains me through each day and will surround me even after death.

For I am convinced that neither death nor life, neither angels nor demons, neither the present nor the future, nor any powers, neither height nor depth, nor anything else in all creation, will be able to separate us from the love of God that is in Christ Jesus our Lord. (Romans 8:38-39)

Crystal lies or a God who loves us? At the door to the New Age, it's a choice we each must make. A rich, full life in Christ is in the balance. And God's love for an eternity.